Rev. David Burke

BERNARDINE REALINO

RENAISSANCE MAN

THE MACMILLAN COMPANY
NEW YORK · BOSTON · CHICAGO
DALLAS · ATLANTA · SAN FRANCISCO

MACMILLAN AND CO., LIMITED
LONDON · BOMBAY · CALCUTTA
MADRAS · MELBOURNE

THE MACMILLAN COMPANY
OF CANADA, LIMITED
TORONTO

BERNARDINE REALINO

RENAISSANCE MAN

FRANCIS SWEENEY, S.J.

NEW YORK

THE MACMILLAN COMPANY

1951

Imprimi potest
James H. Dolan, S.J.
　　Vice-provincial, Province of New England
September 15, 1950

Nihil obstat
　　John M. A. Fearns, S.T.D.
　　Censor Librorum

Imprimatur
　　✠ Francis Cardinal Spellman
　　Archbishop of New York
June 11, 1951

B-Jes
Bs

First Printing

To

ROBERT E. GROSS, M.D.

Cor ad cor dantis cordatum

ACKNOWLEDGEMENTS

So MANY of my fellow Jesuits have aided me in the preparation of this book that I cannot hope to name them all. I have taken advantage of the courtesy shown me at the Boston Public Library, and the libraries of Holy Cross College, Boston College, Harvard University, Yale University and Fordham University. The Library of Congress was also of massive assistance in the search for books.

Chief among my individual creditors are Vincent A. McCormick, S.J., who supplied indispensable biographical material from Rome, and prospered the book with his blessing; Joseph P. Kelly, S.J., Edward G. Callahan, S.J., and the late Robert Swickerath, S.J., who advised me on points of Renaissance history; J. Gerard Mears, S.J., John Louis Bonn, S.J., and Richard G. Philbin, S.J., on whose suggestions I confidently relied in revising the manuscript; S. Oley Cutler, S.J., David C. Bayne, S.J., and Robert F. Drinan, S.J., lawyers and Jesuits all three, who frequently aided me in untangling a *locus desperatus* in the life of the lawyer-saint.

The book could not have been written without the constant cooperation of Charles J. Lewis, S.J., who not only prepared the manuscript and aided me materially by an analysis of Realino's *Commentary*, but also circularized all the public and university libraries of the world where copies of Realino's *Commentary* might be found.

CONTENTS

CHAPTER I · EVERYONE MY BROTHER AND MY FRIEND

From Modena to Bologna the Via Aemilia runs straight as a Roman sword. To the south the undulating foothills of the Apennines begin, and northward lies the vast Lombard plain that extends, a carpet of field and wood, canal and indolent river and clustered towns, to the Alpine frontier. Young Bernardine Realino rode down from Carpi to Modena and then eastward on the ancient Roman way. It was a country of chestnut forests and vineyards, of sparse pastures and tillage, where furrows of wheat alternated with rows of vines in the thrifty Lombard fashion. The muted sunlight of St. Martin's summer made a tawny glory in the harvest fields and the rifled vineyards.

He crossed the Secchia and the Samoggia, little rivers meandering northward to the sea, and almost within sight of Bologna came to the Reno, with its island where the triumvirs, Anthony, Octavius and Lepidus, had divided the world as if it were a round loaf of barley bread. On his right as he came into the environs of the university city rose Monte della Guardia, crowned by the pilgrimage church of Madonna di San Luca, where there was a portrait of the Blessed Mother that was supposed to have been painted by St. Luke. To climb the steep slope to the famous church was a challenge no boy could ignore. Bologna lay below, a hexagonal bulk of city set in its five miles of walls, the narrow streets like cracks in a great cheese. The fortifications had crumbled badly since the stern days three centuries before when the citizens had discharged clouds of arrows and showers of hot pitch on the heads of the soldiers of the Emperor. Beyond the city, forty miles to the east, there was a twinkle of sea.

Far to the west, the way Bernardine had come, the Roman highway lay across the parquetry of fields, a gray thread unraveled from a cloud. By hill and dale and river bank, in forest shadow

1

and the untrammeled sunlight of plowland and fold, past raucous market and droning school, it ran like the road of life, back to the little walled city where he was born.

Carpi in 1530 was living largely on its memories. The struggle between Charles V and Francis I, fought out on the chessboard of Northern Italy, had ended in disastrous checkmate at the siege of Pavia in 1525, when the French forces had been routed and Francis taken to Madrid as a prisoner. Carpi had sided with France, though it is a matter of conjecture just how much help Alberto Pio, Prince of Carpi, had sent to join the polyglot army of Francis about Pavia. At best, only a few culverins or a troop of restless Carpians eager for a taste of war. With the Emperor's victory, the Hapsburg grip was fastened firmly on Northern Italy, not to be shaken off for more than three centuries. Shortly after the battle, Carpi was occupied by an Imperialist force under Prospero Colonna, and then in 1527 it was sold by Charles V to Duke Alfonso I of Ferrara. The Pio family were dispossessed of the city to which they had given two centuries of peace and a modicum of artistic eminence.

The Pii do not pass immediately from view. Alberto Pio, the last lord of Carpi, entered the immediate service of Francis I, and for twenty years had to find the rôle of minor diplomat a dukedom large enough. Others of the family were closely connected with the rise of the new Society of Jesus. Alberto's daughter Caterina was a generous patron of some of Ignatius Loyola's charitable enterprises in Rome. Another daughter, Margherita, was the mother of Blessed Rodolfo Acquaviva, a Jesuit martyr in India. Alberto's nephew, Rodolfo Cardinal Pio, called Cardinal Carpi, was the first and last Cardinal Protector of the Jesuits.

Alberto, a typical Renaissance lord whose gusto and intelligence found each day of life a fresh page to be written in a big, round hand, creditably acted the diverse characters of humanist, diplomat, antiquary, patron of the arts, and smatterer in theology. In his lengthy absences from Carpi he left the management of his properties in the capable hands of Don Bernardine Realino, who held the high office of steward until advanced old age. Don Bernardine's son Francesco entered court service also, but not at Carpi. If he had hoped to inherit his father's office, after serving his cadetship at other courts, the prospect was lost in the downfall of the Pio family. Francesco's life was spent in the service of such personages as Vespasiano Colonna, Luigi Gonzaga, Cosimo dei Medici and Cristoforo Cardinal Madruzzo, Prince-Bishop of Trent.

Though the beauties and the seductions of the Renaissance courts were a familiar spectacle to Francesco Realino, it was at Carpi that he chose his wife. On December 24, 1529, Don Francesco and Donna Elisabetta Bellentani were solemnly engaged, and on the fifth of the following February they were married. The Bellentani were the more distinguished of the two families: humanists and soldiers and an archpriest of Carpi bore the name. The Realino family made up for their lack of pedigree by a fine enthusiasm for hard work and a clear understanding of which side their bread was buttered on. There is no evidence available that they owned property; in 1896 an Italian scholar, Father Ettore Venturi, made an extensive search among notaries' records at Carpi, but was unable to locate the birthplace of the Saint.

Elisabetta's first child was born on December 1, 1530. Francesco was not at home to hear the midwife slap the breath into his baby son and the first indignant wails of the new arrival welcomed with such scant ceremony. The young father was far away discharging his office as master of horse to Luigi Gonzaga, a flamboyant third cousin of St. Aloysius whose *virtù* and *grandezza* had earned him the nickname *Rodomonte*—the Swaggerer. Rodomonte had been serving in the forces of the Prince of Orange, who had been storming the city of Florence. Francesco Realino arrived back in Carpi within a week of his son's birth, and on December 8th the child was carried to the *Sagra*, the Sanctuary, the ancient mother church of Carpi, and christened at the blackened stone font where all the children of the city were baptized.

He was given the names Bernardine and Luigi: Bernardine in honor of St. Bernardine of Siena as well as to give him his grandfather's name; Luigi for Luigi Gonzaga. Francesco Realino would have preferred to put his lord's name first, but Elisabetta's choice prevailed. One of the proud traditions of her family was that Bernardine of Siena had been their guest on his visits to Carpi. The child was christened by Don Antonio dei Lancellotti, the Rector, and had for sponsors the Magnifico Matteo Coccopane and Donna Maria Antonia Muliser. Who they were, or what their connection with the Realini, we do not know. It is glory enough that on this Feast Day of the Immaculate Conception, 1530, they were made spiritual kinsmen of a future saint.

In a memoir of his boyhood which Bernardine wrote at an early age, his enthusiasm for Rodomonte Gonzaga commits him to some boyish superlatives. "He was such a hero both through gifts of soul and strength of body that none of his time could surpass him . . . and perhaps not even the future will have such a one." Though the unparalleled excellence of Rodomonte's gifts seems to have escaped the notice of historians, a moment's glance at the career of the gallant general will serve to suggest what deeds of derring-do stirred Bernardine's boyhood dreams, as well as to show how Francesco Realino earned his soldier's pay.

The son of Ludovico Gonzaga, Marquis of Sabbioneta, Rodomonte served in his early twenties in the army of the Papacy, in the struggles between France and the forces of the Empire and the Holy See. He missed the climax at Pavia because his father had sent him to the court of Charles V in Spain. Reports came back to Sabbioneta of Rodomonte's skill at games and tournaments and his amazing strength demonstrated in vaulting and wrestling. And when the young lad was not flexing his biceps or riding in "the medieval grace of iron clothing," he could turn out quite presentable sonnets.

He visited England with Charles V, and added new particulars to the Rodomonte legend by his courage at boar hunting in Windsor Forest. Ariosto mentions his fame in the *Orlando Furioso*, and Tasso calls him "the great glory of Italy . . . a terror to the foe."

Rodomonte had a command in the imperial forces under the Constable Bourbon at the sack of Rome in 1527. When Bourbon fell in the final assault, Gonzaga led the invaders through the Porta Aurelia. The civilian defenders of the city fled from the walls and the Swiss guards were cut to pieces at the Vatican gates. Pope Clement VII escaped to the shelter of Castel Sant' Angelo while the guns of the fortress boomed defiance to the invaders. One of the gunners was Benvenuto Cellini, who, if his memoir can be believed, proudly demonstrated to His Holiness how he could cut a Spaniard in two with a shot from a falconet. The German, Italian and Spanish mercenaries of the Imperialist army, their pay long overdue, were now beyond control. They proceeded to pillage the Eternal City with a thoroughness and cruelty that the Turk could hardly have surpassed. Though ill with fever, Gonzaga did what he could to protect his friends and for some of them paid the ransom that the soldiers were squeezing out of all the dignitaries in the city. Father Martindale notes, however, that Rodomonte brought home from the sack of Rome many of the treasures which were later housed in the museum at Sabbioneta.

Finally a truce was concluded between the invaders and the imprisoned Pope. When the hapless Clement VII, on the night of December 6, 1527, came out of the fortress under cover of darkness, in the clothes of his major domo, Rodomonte Gonzaga was waiting with thirty horsemen and a troop of arquebusiers to escort the Pope to the papal palace at Orvieto.

The date of Francesco Realino's coming into the employ of Rodomonte is not known. He had served with Vespasiano Colonna, who a year before the sack of Rome had raided the Eternal City, a deed which had caused the Pope to send a punitive force into Colonna territory. In March, 1528, Vespasiano came from the defense of Naples against the French, home to the Colonna stronghold at Pagliano to die. His widow, Giulia Gonzaga, a sister of Rodomonte, called on her brother to defend her property against her rapacious neighbors. With Vespasiano's star fallen, it was a logical time for Francesco to transfer to the employ of Rodomonte. At any rate, whether it was with Colonna or Gonzaga that he passed the half-dozen years before Bernardine's birth, it was a time of swift adventure, raucous with the anger of the artillery and the clashing of the pikes.

Francesco Realino wanted none of it for his son. Many years later, after his father's death, Bernardine wrote to his brother Giambattista:

Among the many obligations that I have to the good memory of my father this is a principal one, that he made it convenient for me to study, and did not wish to send me to court, which he was well able to do because of the familiarity he enjoyed with such eminent princes. May our Lord reward him in heaven, as I trust He does.

Since Don Realino was usually absent from Carpi, Donna Elisabetta, who had none of her husband's taste for courts and camps, exercised the predominant influence in the moulding of Bernardine's character. She was a mild, gentle lady with, however, a will of her own, and a fierce compassion for the poor which she transmitted intact to her son. She loved Bernardine with the special love all mothers have for their first child, and he responded with such affection that even in his old age the thought of her would make the tears come. He was very small when she taught him to say the rosary and to examine his conscience. He went often with her to the Franciscan Church of San Niccolò when the altar was decked for High Mass, the candles like tall sticks with stars on their tops, or at the hour of vespers when the oblique torrents of light from the choir windows made a little Pentecost about the bearded friars singing in the stalls.

Other children blessed the union of Francesco and Elisabetta. Eventually Bernardine had two brothers, Giambattista and Camillo, and three sisters, Elisabetta, Caterina and Camilla. Only Bernardine and Giambattista reached maturity.

Rodomonte Gonzaga's career ended abruptly in 1532. After the devastation of the Eternal City, he was employed in various missions for the Holy See, policing the papal towns in Northern Italy, fortifying the March of Ancona against the Turkish pirates, going to Spain again on an errand to the court. He met death in true Gonzaga style, at the capture of Vicovaro, a town in the Romagna. The attack had gone well: the arquebusiers picking off the defenders on the walls, the artillery hammering down a gate, and then the pikes and calvary going in. At the moment of victory Gonzaga was wounded in the left shoulder by a shot from an arquebus. He was carried to the city hall where he made his confession and dictated his will, one of those long testaments full of minute particulars with which Renaissance lords made their final flourish. All his captains were generously remembered. Then Rodomonte's crowded, restless life was over. He was only thirty-three.

Where Francesco Realino marketed his abilities during the next few years is not known. The statement of some biographers, that he came into the employ of Cristofero Madruzzo on Gonzaga's death, is untenable; Madruzzo was only twenty years old in 1532, and could not have completed his studies at Padua. But seven

years later he had acquired three canonries and he was appointed
Prince-Bishop of Trent in that year. By this time he could main-
tain a household of his own, and no doubt he took Francesco into
his service as master of horse when he was organizing his episcopal
court. Strangely enough, though Francesco Realino seems to have
remained in this post for many years, and to have been solidly
fixed in Madruzzo's esteem, he is not mentioned in the elaborately
detailed diaries of the Council of Trent, where many other gentlemen of the Prince-Bishop's house are named.

Madruzzo was to be made a cardinal four years later, and to
play a major rôle in the Counter-Reformation. He was a man of
considerable culture, and a generous patron of learning and the
arts. Although he was high in the confidence of Charles V, and
was frequently employed on Imperialist diplomatic missions, his
devotion to the Church has never been impugned. His statue,
raised in the last century in his see city, in the Church of St. Mary
Major where the sessions of the Council of Trent were held, is a
testimony to his persevering labor for the success of the Council.

Since Trent was in the Tyrol, beyond the borders of Italy,
and much of the Prince-Bishop's business took him to the north,
the new post would afford Francesco Realino even less opportunity than before to be with his little family in Carpi. Each time
he saw his oldest boy, Bernardine seemed to have grown another
inch. He was old enough now to start his lessons, and Elisabetta
made the decision which is always a wrench at a mother's heart.
Bernardine's first teacher was a relative, Francesco Passi, who
taught him the rudiments of Italian and Latin grammar. It was at
a school kept, by a public subsidy, by a master named Paolo Bres-
ciano that the glory of the Greek burst on his eager mind. Bernardine has left a naive comment on these early school days. He
writes of himself: "From the literary contests which were arranged by the teachers to exercise the pupils, he never came forth
beaten, but not for that reason did he mount to pride or swell
himself vainly or lord it over his companions, but he was always
humble and pleasant and by word and deed he tried to excuse and
commiserate his companions." Any resentment that his classmates
may have felt at being invariably bested by young Realino must
have been dissolved by their appreciation of the open-handed

charity which would make him shake the last *soldo* out of his purse to help a poor student buy books. Bernardine writes of this circumstance: "If I had more money to spend than others, I devoted a good part of it to helping young fellows more talented than I, but who, on account of poverty, were unable to rise, like vines growing on the earth because they have nothing to support them." Though these admissions cause us some surprise, we must concede that everything we know of Bernardine confirms his own frank appraisal of his good qualities. And later events of his student days would blow the feathers of self-complacency out of his cap.

When he had picked up the elements of logic from a certain Doctor Frassetti, who was well-read in philosophy, the Realini judged that their eldest son, now sixteen, had made as much progress as was possible in Carpi. Don Francesco was resolved that his boy should be a scholar and Donna Elisabetta agreed, though there was some reluctance at the thought that Bernardine would be sent far away. It was decided, then, that he should be enrolled at the school in Modena, called a university by courtesy, where he would be only a few miles from home.

On the autumn day in 1546 when Bernardine, in his new broadcloth doublet and hose, rode out of his home city, he left a brilliant reputation behind him, the good report of a boy who had won all the prizes at school, and earned the admiration of his school-fellows as well. "Carpi, where I regard everyone as my brother and my friend," he wrote many years later. Already he had begun to show that genius for friendship which he would later find a danger and then an incalculable advantage. His popularity had come to him through no sacrifice of principle, indeed it came in spite of his allegiance to an ideal which in others might have been repellent. While the other Carpian small fry had been playing ball or hunting hares with the crossbow, or swimming naked as eels in the streams below the town, Bernardine would be lost in the virile grandeur of the *Iliad*, or pulling apart the periods of Cicero and putting them together again in his own tongue.

At Modena Bernardine found himself in contact with the finest elements of Italian culture. The Renaissance, to be sure, had passed its peak, and the first enthusiasm of the rediscovery of antiquity and the vision of the nature and powers of man had somewhat cooled. Or rather, the enthusiasm was directed to more academic goals. In Bernardine's day, to scratch a humanist was usually to find a grammarian or a philologist. The vision had paled to a *wissenschaft* which often did not see the forest for the fascination of measuring all the twigs. Whatever their faults were, the masters at Modena fired the eager youngster from Carpi with a sincere affection for the classics. He became a voracious reader, and it was on the solid nourishment provided by Homer and Plato, Cicero and Sallust that his mind grew and his taste developed. Nor did he scorn, as did so many extreme humanists, the masterpieces in his own language. Later we find him annotating the Italian poems of Petrarch and Bembo.

Among his teachers at Modena were Antonio Bendinelli of Lucca and Luigi Castelvetro. Bendinelli, a professor of grammar, became a close friend of Bernardine, who sought the older man's advice on his literary efforts even after leaving Modena. As for Castelvetro, besides making monumental studies in the development of the Italian language, he was the foremost literary critic of his day.

With the supreme emphasis which the Renaissance placed on linguistic and artistic studies, the formal study of theology had declined. Erasmus had said with some truth that the study of theology and philosophy was more flourishing in his country than in Italy, where it was practically left to a few monks. And Bellarmine was later to complain that there was no country where the priests and bishops were more ignorant than in Italy. Some of the humanists, however, became dabblers in theology, but often enough they went for their inspiration to the paganism of Greece and Rome or to the new religious revolt that was brewing in the towns beyond the Alps.

Heretical ideas were rife in many cities of Northern Italy, Modena among them. Father Girolamo Tiraboschi, in his *Storia della Letteratura Italiana*, quotes Alessandro Tassoni, a contemporary chronicler, on the situation in Modena:

And not only men, of every shade of learning and ignorance, and those who have no knowledge of literature, but even women, whenever an opportunity occurs, in streets, drug-stores or in church, dispute about the faith and law of Christ, and they all recklessly attack the sacred scriptures, quoting Paul, Matthew, John, the Apocalypse and all the Doctors, whom they have never read.

By all accounts the leadership in these garrulous discussions of amateur theologians was taken by the members of a literary academy which had been founded in his own house by Giovanni Grillenzoni, a Modenese physician. Castelvetro, who had translated the works of Melancthon into Italian, eventually became its president. The academicians were especially a thorn in the side of visiting preachers, whose every word they scrutinized and questioned. In 1542 Giovanni Cardinal Morone, Bishop of Modena, wrote that the Dominicans were unwilling to visit Modena any longer because of the persecution they had undergone from the academy.

The state of religion at Modena aroused some concern at Rome and in spite of Castelvetro's assurances of loyalty and that of his companions, a formulary of faith was sent from Rome, and in September of 1542 was solemnly signed by the chief magistrates, the heads of religious houses and other prominent men in the city. Yet the air had not cleared in 1545, the year before Bernardine came to Modena, when Cardinal Morone called the Jesuit theologian, Father Alfonso Salmeron, to Modena to oppose by his preaching the harmful influence of the academy. Salmeron, never a skilled hand at pouring oil on turbulent waters, displeased the Cardinal by the forthrightness of his sermons, and was sent packing out of the diocese. Morone did not lose his regard for the Jesuits, however. They were back in Modena a few years later to found a college.

Castelvetro was riding for a fall, for his Lutheran sympathies were now under the scrutiny of the Roman Inquisition. It was after Bernardine's sojourn at Modena that Duke Ercole II suppressed the academy of Grillenzoni, and at the request of Pius IV, signed a warrant for Castelvetro's arrest for trial in Rome. The humanist fled from Modena and though condemned as a heretic at Rome he was able to enjoy a precarious liberty by a life of wandering. He made a rather pathetic appeal to have his case considered by the Council of Trent, a request that was denied.

Very little is recorded of the classes that Bernardine followed in Modena, but we know that he was constantly in attendance at the academy, where a daily lecture was given on Greek literature and one on Latin. He could not have been a full-fledged academician, entitled to participate in the meetings, until his matriculation at Bologna. Though at seventeen he was more mature than an American lad of twenty, still he was fresh from the grammar school at Carpi. Certainly no suggestion has ever been made that he was infected with the Lutheran virus at Modena. He is one of that faithful majority of whom Tiraboschi writes: "It seems to me that the glory of the Modenese is greater from the greater perils they underwent, and from which they came forth nonetheless with their religion uncorrupted and unchanged." It is only as a man of letters that Castelvetro, in Bernardine's memoir, is termed "*vir ingeniosissimus,*" as indeed he was.

Though the competition was keener than it had been at school in Carpi, Bernardine continued to give a splendid account of himself. Vastly proud of his son, Don Francesco was not at all unwilling to talk about Bernardine's successes. Cardinal Madruzzo was impressed. Though the Prince-Bishop of Trent had become one of the busiest men in Europe, as host to a general council of the Church, he had not abandoned his rôle of Maecenas. Would young Realino care to make his university studies at Pavia, at Madruzzo's expense? Besides the income from his several Tyrolese benefices, the Cardinal had recently received, by favor of Charles V, a grant of two thousand ducats from the Archdiocese of Compostella. Bernardine would not be the only scholar on his remittance list. It was an attractive offer, but Bernardine declined it. He preferred to remain in Modena under the guidance of the professors he so much admired; Bendinelli especially was now his close friend. In the book he published a few years later, Bernardine wrote of his mentor: "I am indebted for whatever I have accomplished in literary studies, if indeed I have accomplished anything, to that eminently wise man, Antonio Bendinelli of Lucca, my teacher."

It was not long before he had cause to regret that he had declined the Cardinal's offer. Several of his classmates thought it a pity that such a charming fellow as Bernardine, with hair like a gold helmet, with a witty tongue and a mind like a sword, should be spending the moonlit spring nights with no more pleasant companions than the big folio volumes of Cicero and Quintilian. They laid plans to bring him out into the brawling currents of night life in a university town.

That not all students came to the universities for sheer love of learning is evident from a contemporary description of the University of Padua: "Gentlemen of all nations come hither in great numbers . . . some coming to study the civill law, others the mathematisches, and Musick, others to ride, to practice the Art of Fencing, and the exercises of dancing and activity, under the most skilfull professors of the Arts, drawn hither for the same reason." And Father Allan P. Farrell, in *The Jesuit Code of Liberal Education,* quotes the observation of a Spaniard, Father Francisco Bordon, who, after teaching at Modena, Ferrara and Bologna just about this time, declared that among Italian youth, "neither modesty nor industry nor fear carries any weight whatever, nor is there any humility nor piety nor any trace or shadow of reverence." With which judgment Father Juan Polanco, Secretary General of the Jesuits, was inclined to agree.

Whether Bernardine lodged at Modena in the house of a relative or with the family of one of the masters, we do not know. At any rate, not much supervision was exercised over him, and he was vastly more free than he had been under the loving but clear eyes of his mother.

There was a gaudy charm about the escapades his friends described: roistering through the town in the outlandish costume of Carnival, relaxing one's mind, stiff as buckram with the starch of too much thinking, in the blissful confusion of wine, or roaring the students' songs in tavern choruses until the bright Italian stars paled or the outraged neighbors went for the police. By degrees he yielded to his comrades' invitations. Of course his studies suffered, and his money vanished so quickly that it seemed to melt in his purse.

Something stopped him in his tracks—a humiliating failure in class, a warning from Bendinelli, or the thought of his mother looking at him with affectionate surprise. He realized the perilous situation he was in; though he had not yet seriously offended God, he saw the inevitable end of the course he was running. St. Francis Xavier, while studying at the University of Paris, had come in the same way to the chasm's lip and turned away. Years later, Realino wrote this comment on the crisis of his youth:

> How great was the mercy God showed me, when, as I was walking on a road so slippery, He sent His angel to warn me of my errors, and drawing me away from the gates of hell, to lead me again into the paths of heaven. It was one of those acts of gentle violence by which we are lovingly compelled to enter into the banquet of the celestial spouse.

A little bewildered by the danger he had undergone, Bernardine saw clearly that if he remained in Modena he might be pulled down again by the thousand Lilliputian ropes of good-fellowship. It would be a hard thing to leave his professors, especially Antonio Bendinelli. But the two years' work in the humanities had prepared him for philosophy, and the study of medicine, which he hoped to make his profession.

He chose the University of Bologna for reasons which now are not clear. To be sure, his fellow Carpian, Iacobo Barigazzi, commonly called Berengarius of Carpi, had been a famous professor of anatomy there. A tradition like that, proudly preserved in the home city, might sway a boy of the hero-worshipping sort in his choice of medical school. Bologna had been the greatest, as it was the oldest university in Italy. Padua now had the foremost medical school in Italy, and in legal studies, at least in civil law, the sceptre had passed to Pavia. An obstacle to the transfer from Modena to Bologna, which was in the States of the Church, was the decree of Duke Ercole II which prohibited any of his subjects from going outside his dominions to study. Through the influence of Cardinal Madruzzo, Francesco was able to obtain a dispensation for his son.

Many times during the next eight years Bernardine would pass through Modena on his journeys between Carpi and Bologna. His departure now was more than a practical solution for a problem he could never untangle by remaining: it was symbolic of a lifetime that would see other resolute leave-takings. As he trussed up boxes of books and manuscripts for the baggage mules, and wadded shirts and doublets and handkerchiefs into his trunk, he was packing away his boyhood too. Whatever his impatience to be gone, he could not omit without awkwardness the ceremony of riding around Modena for the courtesies of farewell—bows and thank-yous and the kissing of hands. Because he was eighteen years old now and a gentleman's son.

FYNES MORYSON, the Cambridge bachelor and indefatigable globetrotter, whose garrulous *Itinerary* is crowded like a canvas of the elder Breughel with the customs and the gossip and local color of Europe of the sixteenth century, describes Bologna just about as Bernardine found it in 1548:

The City is seated in a large plaine, and such is the whole territory, onely on the South-side without the wals lie the Apennine mountaines, which divide Italy almost in the midst, all the length thereof even from Genoa, to the furthest limits of the Kingdome of Naples, bordering upon the sea towards the East. On the same South-side, are the schools of the University, and the monastery of Saint Dominicke, in which is the sepulcher of the said Saint curiously engraven, and of white marble, and under a rich skreene lies the body. . . . [The monastery] hath two foure-square Court yards, with arched Cloysters to walke under, and they be pleasantly planted round about with Cedars, of which they especially esteeme one, planted by the hands of that Saint, who likewise with his owne hand did beautifie a well of water no less esteemed by them. Their publicke Library is much esteemed for many bookes of written hand, wherein they brag to have a Bible written by the hand of Esdras. . . . They have a place given by priviledge to the Dutch for buriall.[1] The building of the City is anticke, and many houses seeme to have beene built by the Lombards. The foundations of the houses are of free stone, and the rest for the most part of bricke, built with arched Cloysters towards the street, under which they walke dry in the greatest raine. The Pallaces of Gentlemen are built towards the street, stately on the inside, but with little shew on the outside, and they all seeme to have beene built of old. The windowes are not glased (which the Venetians brag to be proper to their City, as a thing to be wondered at) but they are covered with paper, whereof part is oyled over . . . The

---

[1] This one of the earliest of those little foreign cemeteries which now hold such poignant interest for tourists. Smollett is buried in one of them at Leghorn, Elizabeth Barrett Browning at Florence, and the acre of England beside the wall of Rome holds the body of Keats and Shelley's heart.

strangers students here call the stately Pallace of Cardinall Caup: the sinnes of the Dutch, as built by the Fines imposed on them.[2]

Through the yawning Porta Sant' Isaia, past the lounging soldiers, Bernardine rode into the exciting world of the most famous university in Italy. It was a larger theater of endeavor than he had known at Modena, for Modena was not a university in the same sense as Bologna, which was a *studium generale*, with faculties in law, theology, medicine and arts. By papal favor Bologna granted its graduates the *ius ubique docendi*, the right to teach in any other university. The term *studium* we may take as synonymous with the modern term *university*.

To understand the milieu in which Bernardine was to live for the next eight years, and by which his whole civic career was to be directed, it is necessary to know something of the constitution of the University of Bologna.

Bononia docet, "Bologna the schoolmaster," was the inscription which the medieval Bolognese stamped on their coins. The motto signified that as other cities had their own special means of sustenance—weaving or leather-working or sea-trading or the manufacture of arms—Bologna's chief industry was the maintenance of schools. This dependence of a city on its schools resulted in a form of university administration which is virtually unknown in English-speaking countries—except perhaps in the daydreams of schoolboys. In the Bologna of medieval times, at least, it was the students, not the professors, who governed the university.

The *universitas* was a guild of students from the ages of seventeen to forty who hired professors to lecture to them. A compelling reason for the guild organization of the students, and their strong insistence on their autonomy, lay in the nature of medieval citizenship. In a day when Italy was a mosaic of fiefs and republics, with no common citizenship, a traveler was often at the mercy of the city where he was sojourning. There was a different and more lenient law for the citizen than for the stranger. (Which

---

[2] This is undoubtedly the palace of Lorenzo Cardinal Campeggio, who was appointed Bishop of Bologna by Clement VII. In this palace were held the Bolognese sessions of the Council of Trent. The "Dutch" are of course the members of the German nation in the University.

also explains why banishment was a more severe penalty than it would be today).

By threats of corporate removal to other cities, the students were able to exact many concessions, even a quasi-citizenship, from the municipal authorities. Since university buildings were a relatively late development, and the lectures were given in a room in the professor's house or in a hired apartment, it would not be difficult for a large section of the student body to pack up and be gone overnight. In the first quarter of the thirteenth century there were three such mass migrations from the city.

Papal and imperial favor added to the students' prerogatives. In the twelfth century the Emperor Frederick Barbarossa decreed that all foreign students should have safe conduct for journeying to Bologna, residing there and returning home; they were exempted from the usual civil jurisdiction and given the right of being judged by the master of their school or by the Bishop of Bologna. When disputes between the city and the university were referred to the Holy See, the Popes, many of them Bolognese alumni, usually decided in favor of the students. With this accretion of power to the students' guilds, the lot of the professors became more and more abject. Canon Rashdall, the great historian of the medieval universities, does not hesitate to say, "The students did no doubt at last succeed in reducing the Masters to an almost incredible servitude."

The guilds of law students held the commanding position in the university, and were the most numerous group. The original legists' guilds, whether four or more, were united since the middle of the thirteenth century into two great guilds or *universitates*, the Cis-Alpine guild for Italians and the Trans-Alpine for students from other countries. These were divided into nations, the Italian guild into Lombards, Tuscans and Romans; the Trans-Alpine guild listed at various times sixteen nations, including Spanish, French, English, Polish, Flemish, German, Savoyard and Hungarian students. A single guild for students of medicine and of arts, which was largely regarded as a preparation for medical studies, was a late development. Since the theological faculty was subject to the Bishop of Bologna and not to the students, as were the other faculties, there was no guild of theologians.

Each national group elected a delegate to a council that chose a rector for each of the two legist guilds and the arts and medicine guild. The rectors and the council were the ordinary executive body of the university. In Bernardine's time the number of rectors had been reduced to one, who was required to be a cleric. This meant only that he had received tonsure from his bishop. A fantastic quantity of dignity adhered to the office of rector. A visiting cardinal who would rank with the princes of the blood in any court in Christendom, would be obliged to yield precedence to a Bolognese rector, who might be a freshly tonsured law student of twenty-four.

The supreme legislative body of the university was the *congregatio*, the assembly of all the students except citizens of Bologna. Since the faculty were the employees of the students, the statutes passed by the *congregatio* were aimed principally at the foibles of the professors. They were obliged to swear obedience to the students' rector and to obey the regulations of the *congregatio*. Professors who were late or absent without the consent of their pupils, or who prolonged their lectures one minute after the dismissal bell had rung, were subject to a fine. Difficulties which were presented to a professor in class were to be answered immediately and not postponed to the end of the lecture. A committee of students called the *denunciatores doctorum* observed the conduct of the professors and reported any irregularities to the rector.

The only prerogative of the professors which student control did not touch was the right to pass judgment on the fitness of candidates for the academic degrees. The sole restriction laid on this right of the professors was the statute of the university which required that, in the final examination for the doctorate, the professors treat the candidate as if he were their own son—a sentiment which might well be urged on professors everywhere. To safeguard their own futures, the professors usually required of the graduates an oath that they would not teach in Bologna.

On that autumn day in 1548, when Bernardine came to Bologna, many of the characteristics of the medieval university were still intact. And the democratic organization of the *studium* was to endure in some form for two centuries more. True, the autonomy

of the students' guilds had declined, a fact which may be traced
to the incorporation of Bologna in the States of the Church in
1506, and the growth of residential colleges. There were several
of these—charitable foundations for poor students or national colleges—but a large proportion of the students still lived in freely
associated groups who rented their own houses, and made their
own arrangements for food and furnishings and the hire of servants. Bernardine lived in a rented house of this sort, in lodgings
which, his memoir hints, were quite comfortably furnished. Only
one of his *socii*, his fellow-lodgers, is known, Domenico Pettorali,
who may have been with him in Modena. And even Domenico
is remembered only because of his anxiety for his friend's health.

When Messer Bernardine had paid his lecture fee and had sworn
obedience to the rector, his name was entered on the member-
ship roll of the guild of artists and medical students. In his new
scholar's *cappa*, the black cloak which the university statutes required him to wear, he went about the city on equal terms with
any of the six thousand students from half the countries of Europe
who poured into the university quarter for the opening of the
scholastic year. Prowling through the university section, which
occupied about one-fourth of the area within the city walls, he
found that it was really a "Latin Quarter" for the various races
conversed in Latin, each nationality imparting its own nasal or
guttural tone to a patois that was already barbarous enough.
Blonde Germans and dark-skinned Spaniards rode in from the city
gates with their baggage mules plodding behind them. Hungar-
ians and Romans joined the crowds at the stationers' stores where
the legal and medical texts were sold. Professors in their furred
gowns exchanged dignified greetings with their students. Jews in
yellow caps, soldiers with heavy pikes and sweeping mustaches,
friars with shaven heads, fish-peddlers, barbers, muleteers, mingled
in the tide of humankind that flowed along the arcaded sidewalks.

On the feast of St. Martin of Tours, November 11, 1548, the
Solemn Mass of the Holy Ghost marked the opening of the uni-
versity year. The Mass, celebrated by the Dominicans at San
Domenico, was the occasion for parading all the symbols of glory
which were the spoils of the university's centuries of existence.
Bernardine would be a little dazzled by the pomp of the academic

procession, with the professors of the four faculties marching into the choir of the church in purple gowns with hoods of miniver; the university beadles carrying their heavy ceremonial maces, escorting the rector, magnificent in robes of scarlet and gold.

Classes began each day at seven when the bell of the Cathedral of San Pietro rang for Mass. Bernardine came in the gray light of early morning through the swarming streets, clothed in the long scholar's gown which was like a loose cassock, with a row of buttons at the throat. The *tramontana,* the cold wind that drove down from the Alps, made a heavy woolen cloak and cap almost a necessity. When *La Scolara*, the great school bell in the Cathedral tower sent its bronze summons down the *Mercato di Mezzo*, the avenue of the schools, the streets were swept clean of laggard students as if with a broom. In the rented house near the portico of the Church of Santa Maria della Morte, where the philosophy classes met, Maestro Anton Francesco Fava ascended the rostrum, opened the thick volume of Aristotle and began to discourse on the beauties of the syllogism.

The first lecture lasted for two hours, and there were two more lectures in the afternoon, and possibly classes in auxiliary subjects late in the morning. Thursday was always a holiday unless a festival recognized by the University occurred in the same week. The long vacation began on September 7th and lasted for two months. There was a holiday also of two weeks at Easter, three weeks at Carnival and ten days at Christmas.

For the first three years of his sojourn at Bologna, Bernardine followed the lectures of the faculty of arts and medicine. The curriculum was based on the philosophy of Aristotle, divided by years into logic, metaphysics and ethics. Some attention was given as well to the studies of the ancient *quadrivium*, as handed down from the ancient Roman schools: arithmetic, geometry, music and astronomy. That medicine also claimed part of Bernardine's time is evident from some notes on anatomy found among his papers. For the present, the larger emphasis was on philosophy, and with this arrangement he was well content, though there is no doubt that he was committed heart and soul to a career in medicine. He notes in his memoir:

I was diligent in attending classes in the philosophy of Aristotle, though refreshing from time to time my spirit with studies more pleasant; and all my nights I devoted to medicine, to which I wished to dedicate myself entirely. For indeed it is a noble art and one worthy of a man of ample talent, but it has the appearance of a body without a soul unless philosophy breathe life into it.

These "studies more pleasant" were the classics for which his ardent devotion had been kindled by Bendinelli and Castelvetro. In literature he found the low door in the wall that led to lawn-lapt gardens with vistas of green and violet mountains and castles perched on tufts of landscape. "For since there are many things to which the mind can devote itself," he wrote, "and each one makes his own choice, I followed the humanities, as they are called, so that I turned to them as often as I could steal some leisure from the more onerous study of Aristotle."

If he had made his first acquaintance with the academy movement at Modena, Bernardine now became an active academician. He was received as a member of one of the Bolognese academies and it was partly in this connection that his reputation as a litterateur was made.

The large number of these literary discussion groups which sprang up all over Italy in the fifteenth and sixteenth centuries were a potent force in the progress of the Renaissance. In the spread of the humanistic cult of antiquity Rashdall assigns them even more credit than the universities. The first of them seems to have been that founded at Rimini towards the close of the fourteenth century by the poet Jacobo Allegretti. Others were founded at Rome, Naples and Venice, for the study of poetry and other literary genres, and eventually for philosophy.

In the sixteenth century every city of any notable size had its academy, and the character of the organization had changed. Italian literature was now studied as well as classical letters. Instead of a rather dry program of orations, poems and critical essays, the academies enlivened their meetings with plays and banquets. Women were admitted as members. The endless discussion of love, which wafts the stench of stale perfume through the pages of Italian literature of the sixteenth century, found its place in the sessions of the academies. Some of the leading figures in Italian literature engaged in this dalliance, arguing such propositions as, "That man in his nature loves more intensely and with greater constancy than woman"; and "That it is more difficult to love and pretend not to love than not to love and pretend to love."

With the frivolous turn the academies had taken, the groups adopted fantastic names. Thus there were the *Frozen Ones* and the *Astonished Ones* of Bologna, the *Stunned* of Siena, the *Insipid* of Ferrara, and the *Enchained*, the *Bewildered*, the *Damaged* and the *Obtuse*. And the individual members took fictitious names. St. Charles Borromeo, in the academy he founded at the Vatican, wished to be called *Chaos*.

What Bernardine's pseudonym was, or the name of the academy he joined is not known. Amid the crowds of genuine scholars and poseurs, of poets and literary exhibitionists, he kept his quiet confidence in his own powers, and a wariness inspired by the lesson he had learned at Modena. But now it was a more subtle temptation that beset him. The academies were to a large extent mutual admiration societies, and there was much to admire in Realino's intimate acquaintance with the poets of classical times and of his own Italy. He was developing as well a flair for turning out sound, well-tooled sonnets, or crackling epigrams. He could compose odes to read aloud for the approval of an audience which might be applauding the cut of the young man's hair or the color of his doublet as much as the quality of his verse. In a word, he was a poet when verse-writing was not at all a rare accomplishment among educated men, and as Father Giuseppe Germier, his latest Italian biographer, remarks, "It was enough in those times to have a talent a little exceeding mediocrity to feel oneself a litterateur and a poet."

None of Bernardine's extant poems exceeds mediocrity, and there is no indication that his lost manuscripts would enlarge his fame. As a scholar and critic his reputation is on firmer ground, yet even here he was never recognized as of first or second rank. Father Tiraboschi's *Storia della Letteratura Italiana* lists him among the minor luminaries of the High Renaissance:

Realino, in the thirty-four years before he entered religion, gave many evidences of a ready and flexible talent, whether at Modena, where he frequented the academy of Castelvetro, whether at Bologna and Ferrara, where he devoted himself to quite profound studies, whether at Milan and Naples, where he held several honorable positions, and still wrote many works of different types, which can be found listed in the biography written by Father Fuligatti.

Bernardine himself destroyed as many of his manuscripts as he could reach, before his entrance into the Society, after first resolving to send them to his father. After his death, the Jesuits collected some of his writings, but much of this material was lost in the confusion following the suppression of the Society of Jesus in 1773. Only one poem survives which can be ascribed with certainty to the early period of Realino's life. It was written as an introduction to a rather dry little book, *Quaestiones Legales*, a commentary on certain cases in civil and canon law taken from the lectures of Iacobo Butrigarius, a famous legal scholar who had flourished at Bologna in the fourtecnth century. The book was published at Bologna in 1557, the year after Bernardine had left the city. Nothing could be more prosaic than his thirteen Latin lines, and the translator must be pardoned if he restores them, after four centuries in the awkward posture of verse, to their native prose:

BERNARDINE REALINO OF CARPI, ATTORNEY-AT-LAW

To the Reader

In this book are made available to you for the first time a few of the cases of Butrigarius. That name should be the best whet to your enjoyment (for who does not know the ability of that man, a genius by all confessed, whom even Bartolo took for teacher?) Yet I will add this in all frankness: it well may be that you will find some problems here explained which up to now had gone unsolved. When Butrigarius takes a case in hand, he finds a solution and ends the dispute, so that you might think that this book came from the hand of the Goddess of Justice herself.

Read, then, if you are wise. More of the same sort will follow, unless you fail to welcome these selections.—But who would not welcome what is useful and good?

The book may be found in the Harvard Law School Library. It seems to have eluded the search of Bernardine's European biographers.

In his *Bibliothèque de la Compagnie de Jésus*, Carlos Sommer-vogel, S.J., lists the lost manuscripts of Realino. Those that can be safely ascribed to the university years show the wide gamut of his literary interests. There was a translation of the *Odyssey*, and of Aristophanes' *Plutus*, fringed with notes and mythological erudition; studies in the sonnets of Petrarch and Bembo; commentaries on the *Conspiracy of Cataline* of Sallust and the *Elegies* of Cornelius Gallus. Also a Latin poem on the joining of wisdom and power, entitled *Pallas Armata;* various translations of Greek poets; two notebooks full of Italian verses and critical judgments written down on various occasions; a collection of descriptive passages from Greek and Latin authors, in imitation of a book of *Emblems* by Andrea Alciato, who was one of his professors at Bologna. Bernardine's memoir we have already mentioned; it was written in Latin in two parts, and recorded the events in his life up to the age of twenty-one. All these manuscripts, as well as those written during Bernardine's years of government service, are presumed to have perished, except for a fragment of the memoir, which was reprinted in the *Summarium* of the canonization process.

Out of the precious *juvenilia*, one work achieved the specious immortality of publication as a book. While Bernardine was still studying in Modena, he began a rather ambitious project for his eighteen years: a commentary on *The Marriage of Peleus and Thetis*, the longest poem of Catullus. In the midst of his arts course at Bologna, he sent the finished manuscript to Antonio Bendinelli, who advised him to publish it. Bernardine was twenty-one when the book came from the press of Anselmo Giaccarelli. The quarto volume of 130 pages is a worthy example of the art of the Renaissance bookmaker; a recent monograph on Giaccarelli lists this book as among the best of the products of that excellent printer, who holds his own honorable place in the fascinating history of the presses of the Renaissance. The title page of the book is in clean Roman capitals, and the body of the text in a face that looks to one amateur eye like Aldine italic, but which an expert calls cursive. The printing is disposed between wide margins on a page whose beauty and spacious order still witness to the craftsman's intelligence.

It was a handsome trophy to send off by the first post to Bendinelli, to his family in Carpi, and to Cardinal Madruzzo, for the book was dedicated to the Prince-Bishop. The obeisance to the Cardinal, made in a graceful address at the beginning of the book, is repeated at the end of the commentary to introduce an appendix entitled *"Adnotationes in Varia Scriptorum Loca"*—Notes on Selected Passages in Certain Authors—and again in a curtain speech at the end of the book.

In offering the book to "Christophero Madrutio, Amplissimo Cardinali Tridentino," Bernardine gives his reasons for the dedication:

Behold, illustrious Cardinal, your own Realino's little gift, a thing so little worth, I know well, as not to be appropriately given to one of your stature; nor is it such as I would want to offer you, but it is presented just that you may have some concrete token of my respect for you. At this season you expect no more from me than that, nor can I give more. . . .

And so with a benign heart and smiling face accept this work, whatever its quality may be, as your protégé's first-fruits, which are indeed owed to your kindness, as gold to the sun, as silver to the moon, as brass to Venus, as iron to Mars, and as to Apollo of the Muses whatever fruit grows in their gardens. Be like that king among kings (I speak of Artaxerxes), who once on a journey, when someone cupped his hands and offered him a drink from a neighboring stream, gladly drank, valuing more the love the heart gave than the lowly quality of the giver or his gift. Once I know that this work of mine has not been found displeasing in your sight, I shall address myself with fresh energy to bring other projects to completion. *Vale.*

On the last page of the book a postscript renews the dedication:

Such, illustrious Cardinal, are the first-fruits of my garden which I would dedicate to you. They are tasteless to be sure, but if you look at the goodwill of the giver, you will not despise them. So take them in good part, I beg of you, and with God's help, in time there will be better offerings to please you. *Vale.*

The reference to the Cardinal as Realino's benefactor leaves little doubt of the practical assistance given by the busy prelate during the university years. Whether Bernardine's fees at Bologna were met entirely by Madruzzo cannot be determined; it seems unlikely in view of later allusions to the kindness of his father in providing so generously for his education. In any case, the dedication to the powerful churchman was a bid for future patronage.

Catullus's *The Marriage of Peleus and Thetis* is sometimes called an epithalamium, or nuptial song, but seems to be more properly termed an epyllion, a miniature epic. It is a marvelous little tour-de-force, full of pictures of blue sea, the pillared shadow of pine groves and the flowering fields of Thessaly. Bernardine's commentary is a collection of miscellaneous information, literary, historical, philosophical—even medical—strung on the framework of a phrase-by-phrase annotation of the poem. Figures of speech are indicated, parallel passages cited from a great number of authors (Germier counted 120), and variant readings are given and the commentator's choice defended. The appendix, *Adnotationes,* contains observations on sixteen passages in other authors, illuminated by the same sort of erudition. A few of the chapter headings will suggest the manner of the work: "Two verses of Propertius construed, and a light thrown on Ovid"; "A word corrected in Propertius and Ovid"; "A passage in Juvenal, and other matters worthy of note"; "On the quartan fever, and a passage in Cicero construed."

The book is a striking tribute to Bernardine's industry and his wide context of reading. The authors cited range through the whole field of the Greek and Latin classics, and include as well the Old Testament, Jerome, Augustine, Avicenna, Galen, Erasmus and some of Bernardine's contemporaries. Like many another author, he found his book a new way to pay old debts, and he kisses his hand, with graceful Ciceronian superlatives, to Francesco Passi, his first teacher, to Bendinelli, Castelvetro, Giovanni Grillenzoni, and to his uncle, Francesco Bellentani of Carpi.

Whatever small esteem the commentary once commanded, its value now is chiefly to show the measure in which Bernardine Realino was a man of his time—or rather a young man of his time, for we must not forget that he was only twenty-one. We better understand the stature of the saint he became when we consider what he was at twenty-one, and what ambitions he gave up when the call of Christ came to him, a rich young man who did not turn away. He had the Renaissance man's cult of fame, for he says in his second address to Madruzzo, "As Pliny teaches, I would leave something after me, as evidence that once I lived." And though he allows that, because of his youth, he cannot pretend to a perfectly formed critical faculty, he lectures Catullus for the impropriety of extending a digression to unwarranted length:

This is a digression, concerning which Horace and the rhetoricians have laid down rules; but their teaching is that these digressions must not be too long. And in the same terms this teaching is found in many places in the writings of Sebastiano Corradi, a man of great authority and a firm friend of mine. Now Catullus, though he is called Learned almost as a middle name, is usually censured for this passage where he goes off on the story of Theseus and Ariadne as if he had forgotten his main argument, and *mehercle,* he is so long about this digression that it is hard to find a word to say in his defense.

A quantity of *odium litterarium* was part of the common baggage of scholarship in those days. To have killed one's man in a duel of pamphlets was a prized distinction, which both Castelvetro and Bendinelli had won. Bernardine was not averse to this elegant acrimony. A chapter in the *Adnotationes* entitled, "A Note on Angelus Politianus," brings an echo of small-arms fire from the literary coteries, and offers an example of the verve and economy of Realino's best prose:

I know that there will be those who will sharpen their malicious teeth on me and my writings, to prevent my departing by a finger's breadth from their own manner of scholarship. Realino, these envious ones say, only fights in the shadow, and looks for fame by wrestling with ghosts. I would have them know that if I do not confine myself to writers of the first rank, I have neither hatred nor vain ambition as my motive. Nor is there anything in my character or habits to prompt me to yap like a noisy dog at those whose shades I venerate. But whatever we write is to be accepted in the spirit which seeks the benefit of all; a friend of Socrates, a friend of Plato, yes—but above all a friend of truth.

The *Adnotationes* eventually received a wider circulation than the rest of the book by reason of their being reprinted by Janus

Gruter in an early edition of his *Thesaurus Criticus*, a seven-volume rummage of oddly assorted lore, published in Frankfort volume by volume, from 1602 to 1634. The title page of the vast work might have been composed by Polonius: *Lampas, sive fax artium liberalium, in quo infinitis locis theologorum, jurisconsultorum, medicorum, philosophorum, oratorum, historicorum, poetarum, grammaticorum, scripta supplentur, corriguntur, illustrantur, notantur . . . ex otiosa bibliothecarum custodia erutos, et foras prodire iussus, a Jano Grutero.*

As for the original book published so proudly in 1551, Bernardine included it in the sweeping sacrifice that he made on his entrance into the Jesuits. Sommervogel notes: "*L'édition de 1551 est très-rare; l'auteur détruisait lui-même tous les exemplaires qui tombèrent entre ses mains.*" Some escaped the flames; the original printing cannot have been large. After inquiries made in all the important public and university libraries in the world, locations can now be given for twenty-two copies, undoubtedly the majority of those extant. There is no available way of searching private collections. The book is found in Realino's own university city at the library of the university, and the Archiginnasio; in Rome at the Vatican, the National Library, the University of Rome, and the Jesuit archives; at the National Library in Naples; at the Trivulziana Library and the Brera in Milan, the Library of St. Mark in Venice; the Este Library in Modena; the Swiss National Library in Berne; the university libraries at Freiburg and Göttingen; the Public Scientific Library in Berlin; the Bavarian National Library in Munich. The Bibliothèque Nationale in Paris has two copies, and there are single copies at the Bodleian, at Cambridge University and at the Rylands Library in Manchester. The only copy located in the western hemisphere is at the University of Chicago.

So the book which was to bear witness to future generations that once Bernardine Realino lived, and whose handsome pages he would have destroyed utterly when his ambitions changed and he chose another goal, still carries his name honorably before the world in many foreign places he never saw. Yet it would have gone down long since into the common humus of forgotten books, of interest only to a rare scholar or antiquary, unless God in the divine humor of the gospel paradox had not given back in sanctity the renown freely sacrificed. Bernardine's career of scholar and versemaker serves now to define and accentuate by contrast the glory of his larger achievement. It is a merciful disposition of Providence that we are not all poets; it is a tragedy—the only one, Léon Bloy says—that we are not saints.

It is in Bernardine's letters that the character of the man is brought into focus as in a burning glass. There we discover his gratitude and affection for his friends, headlong enthusiasm that gave winged sandals to all his resolutions, faith and childlike piety mingled with the critical instincts of the scholar, above all the *italianità* that crackles and sings amid the flowers of rhetoric and the ripple of the sentences. We must confess that in his lack of humor, Bernardine took the color of his time. Sixteenth-century Italy took itself very seriously, and the medieval laughter of Christian men was a rare commodity in the professor-ridden world of footnotes and flattering sonneteers and the carpet gallants of the drawing room. Yet Bernardine could not have been quite a glum young man—he had so many friends. And we must allow for the limitations of biographies in which objectivity has played a losing game against edification.

If he lost his sense of humor in the university and the academies, he would find it again in the hundredfold which is the sublime usury of those who make themselves beggars for God's sake. Then Bernardine would laugh at the world, and pray for the world, laugh at himself and flog his body like a stubborn packmule. But that was long after his philosophy days, when all Lecce opened its heart to the smiling Saint as it opened its windows to the sunlight.

CHAPTER III · FLIGHT

WHILE Bernardine was laying siege to knowledge and fame at the university, in quiet Carpi the clear, steadfast flame of Elisabetta Realino's life began to flicker and fail. At the beginning of 1550 an urgent message called Bernardine back to Carpi, where his mother was suffering from a heart ailment. For some months he spent much of his time with her, getting in the way of the servants, anxiously questioning the doctor, lingering at the bedside with his eyes on his mother's calm face.

Donna Realino had regained some strength by the end of the summer, and at the beginning of the school year she sent Bernardine back to the university as firmly and as cheerfully as she had packed him off to Modena years before. He went reluctantly and with a drop of fear in his heart like a bead of fire. Hardly had he settled himself for his final year of philosophy when, on November 24, 1550, word came that Elisabetta Realino was dead.

Work and prayer were oil and wine for the wounds of grief in the bitter months after his mother's death. He turned with deeper need and a new sincerity to the devotions he had learned as a child, particularly prayer to Our Lady and to Christ in the Blessed Sacrament, and the daily examination of conscience he had made since he was very young. He remembered poignantly now, when he made frequent visits to the church of San Michele al Bosco, how his mother had taken him to the Franciscan church in Carpi, when he and she were alone together, the father absent on his expeditions, the younger children as yet only a hope. The wise and friendly advice of one of the Olivetan monks at San Michele, a fellow Carpian, helped the grieving lad through the bitter time.

It was in San Michele or in another of Bologna's numerous churches that Bernardine first saw the lady who was to take his mother's place as the most powerful earthly influence on his life. They say he was struck by her beauty, or by her extreme recollection, a sharp contrast to the proverbial nonchalance of Italians in church. Somehow they met, and Bernardine was delighted to find that she was as richly endowed with the mind's treasures as with the beauty of eyes and lips and hair. She was well-read in philosophy, and could reply with gay, musical verses to the sonnets in which Bernardine expressed his admiration for her. One early biographer declares that there was no trace of impropriety in these poems—which no one can doubt. Another says that they were all on religious subjects, which is drawing the long bow of edification too far.

She was one of those lettered ladies of the Renaissance who had read their Latin and Greek, and even philosophy and theology, as deeply as their brothers and husbands, and who by sheer force of genius had won acknowledgement of intellectual equality in a society that was still very much a man's world. Vittoria Colonna, Giulia Gonzaga, Tarquinia Molza were some of the more famous of them. Bologna has had its share of bluestockings, some of whom have occupied chairs in the university. Thus in the fourteenth century, a certain Novella d'Andrea professed canon law; so remarkable was her beauty that she lectured from behind a curtain. At a much later date, there were female professors in mathematics, anatomy and Greek.

The riddle in the life of Bernardine Realino is the identity of the girl who captured his heart as surely as Rodomonte Gonzaga had ever taken a town. Realino refers to her as Chloris, the name of the Greek goddess of flowers. It is a good conjecture that the name is a literary pseudonym, even the title used by the young lady as member of an academy. But at a time when children were receiving at the font names likes Ascanius, Hercules, Hippolyta, Olympia and Parthenia, we cannot be sure that Chloris was not her baptismal name.

The problem is further complicated by Bernardine's mention of another name. In his *Adnotationes* he says naively: "We know also that Ovid, in the second book of his *Amores*, commemorates the death of his Corynna's parrot. And after his example I myself once mourned the death of my Chrysia's nightingale." Tiraboschi, in his *Biblioteca Modenese*, cites two epigrams addressed to Bernardine, written by Pietro Antonio Montagnana, Professor of

Belles Lettres in Bologna, on the death of a certain Chrysia whom Realino loved. Only the shorter of the epigrams is quoted:

> Why do you look for tears in others? Why weep yourself?
> Because Chrysia seemed to die, Realino?
> Her substance is changed to something better than it was—
> Believe me, she could not really perish.
> Dash away your tears, then, and lift up your heart:
> For Chrysia who was mortal is become a goddess.

Tiraboschi speculates that Chloris and Chrysia ("golden one" in Greek) are the same person, and the probability is a strong one: both died young. Whoever Chloris may have been, there was soon no question of Bernardine's total devotion to her. Not all of the Saint's biographers have thought it best to mention Chloris—as if a romance could detract from the glory of Bernardine Realino's life. This is in contrast to the frankness of Bernardine's own memoir. "This lady, as beautiful as she is good, and pure—a lady second to none in prudence." With perfect simplicity he owned his admiration for her, and he called her "*mia elettissima donna*," "the lady of my heart," and he added, "I loved her with a rare affection, even to the extent that I could consider myself happy only when I could satisfy her wishes."

When Bernardine completed his philosophical and pre-medical studies in 1551, he planned to devote his whole time to medicine, which would involve gaining much practical experience in dissection room and hospital and accompanying physicians on their rounds. It was Chloris who changed the whole current of his life. She had decided that his talents were more suited to a legal career, and she urged him now to enroll for the lectures of the faculty of law. Bernardine remained unconvinced. The change would mean that much of the preparatory study he had made during the past three years would be wasted. The law course at Bologna required five or six years of hard work and he was reluctant to undertake it. But he yielded to Chloris' strongest argument: "Nothing is difficult to one in love." It was the authentic language of the love-struck Renaissance courts, and Realino was as susceptible to it as any.

So for the love of the lady of his heart, he entered the guild of the law students and began to attend the lectures in civil and canon law, which were being given at that time in a building adjacent to the Church of San Petronio. On the first day of the autumn term of 1551, an incident happened which impressed him so forcibly that he recorded it, embroidered with classical allusions, in his memoir:

In the house I rented there was a canary that sang tunefully and almost spoke. Some days before, he had muted his singing as if he were sick at heart or recalled the sad fate of Theseus. When I was on the point of setting foot outside the house and betaking myself to the public lecture-hall, while I was passing through one of the tastefully-furnished rooms, in which the cage hung from a beam, the canary began to sing sweetly and to flutter his wings as if he wished to greet me. I stopped, a little bewitched, I frankly admit, by the unwonted beauty of the fragile little bird's song, and I stood whistling softly in imitation of the tune, to see whether in some way he would understand me—such a spell the thing had cast on me.

At length, when I turned to go, he fell into silence. When I turned back, he began to sing; when I went away, he stopped. And so it went for three days: when I was present, he made merry, if I did not come he mourned in his cage. Such things, I told myself, do not happen without the permission of heaven. Could the canary be a herald of good fortune? For if, in the Sicilian campaign, a fish glided out of the water and came to the feet of Augustus, who was walking on the strand, as a sign that they who then ruled the sea would be prostrate at Caesar's feet —could all this be an omen for me? Alas for our false human hopes and idle dreams.

Francesco Realino heartily seconded his son's change of plans and willingly provided the rather large sum Bernardine needed for textbooks. In his service at the courts of Italian princes he had seen the power wielded by chancellors and ambassadors, and now that the flood of violence and anarchy which had reached its height in the Sack of Rome was receding, careers in government and diplomacy would hold out even richer rewards.

With the intellectual renaissance of the twelfth century the old legal codes, that had been the norms of Europe's governance in the days of the Caesars, came out of the libraries and were studied with an eye to the political organization of the Italian city-states. They were appealed to by both sides in the struggles for power between Emperor and Pope. *Ecclesia vivit lege Romana* was a common saying in the schools, but if the Church poured her marvelous life into the forms of Roman law, as she did into so many molds left from the pagan world, it was to change and smooth the original harsh matrix. Side by side with the teaching in civil law grew the study of canon law, founded on the compilation of decretals made by Gratian, the Camaldolese monk. Since Church and State were united in a comradeship of power, law students frequently made their studies in both laws and received their doctorates *in utroque jure*.

The revival of interest in Roman jurisprudence had begun at Bologna in the twelfth century, when Irnerius, the first of the Bolognese commentators, began to teach civil law. When in the following century a chair of canon law was founded, Bologna was quickly recognized as the first law school in Europe, and the work of the *glossatores*, the Bolognese doctors of the law, gave the university a vast influence on the development of the whole law of western Europe.

Though Pavia now excelled Bologna as a school of civil law, a Bolognese doctorate still carried with it a large quantity of prestige. But it was a vast field that Bernardine must traverse before he could receive the doctor's biretta. The prospect of five more years of early morning classes and long hours of study at the legal texts was discouraging to one who had set his heart on a medical career. But there were Chloris' words sounding in his ears, "Nothing is difficult to one in love," and there was Chloris herself, to shore up his sagging resolution with her smiles and her light hand upon his arm and her cheerful certainty that she knew his abilities better than he did.

Bernardine soon found himself fascinated by the practical appeal of legal studies.[1] After the dry dialectics of Aristotle he was grateful for the constant reference that the law made to the varieties of concrete human experience. Besides studying the codes of Roman and ecclesiastical law, he dipped into political economy,

[1] One of Realino's teachers was Mario Sozzini, called Socinus, of Siena, who was senior professor of civil law at Bologna. Socinianism, the Antitrinitarian heresy that arose in the sixteenth century, owes its name to his son and grandson, Lelius and Faustus Socinus.

reading especially the treatises on political and social organization
of Plato and Aristotle. That he had set as his goal a career in government
service rather than practice in the law courts is evident
from a passage in his memoir:

I was at that time an ambitious fellow—and this is a vice, but as
Sallust says, not far from virtue, and Socrates praises it in young men—
and I admit that there shone before my mind that alluring hope by
which the Emperor Justinian, at the beginning of his *Institutiones*, entices
his students, namely, that it crowns all the work of the law to
address oneself to the governance of the republic.

Whether it was because of this ambition or from sheer passionate
love of learning, Bernardine now lengthened the time he spent
at his desk. He even went to the extreme of bringing a book to
his meals and reading while the food grew cold. Finally he decided
to come to the dining room only once a day and his friend
Domenico Pettorali made it his business to see that Bernardine at
least took one meal in twenty-four hours. Not much account
seems to have been made of breakfast at this time. And even today
the tourist who is accustomed to a hearty American breakfast
may find the Italian *colazione* of a roll and coffee not very
filling.

We have the impression that he did not find literature as much
of a need and an escape as he had during his years as a philosophy
student, though it was far from being neglected. His humanistic
studies had brought him recognition which would have turned
many a young man's head, and for all we know, it may have had
that effect on Bernardine. Several times he rode down to Ferrara,
thirty-four miles away, on errands for his father. The mingled
tyranny and munificence of the Este rule had made Ferrara the
first modern city in Europe, with broad streets and squares, and
palaces standing in spacious grounds. The Este Dukes, for all the
ruthless ducat-cadging of the tax-collectors, were regarded by
the people almost as demi-gods; and this though the dungeons of
the Este citadel reeked with the blood of murdered sons and
wives. John Addington Symonds remarks, "It would be difficult
to give any adequate idea of the frequency of wife-murders in
the higher ranks of society at this epoch, the second half of the
sixteenth century."

Like most of the Renaissance lords, the Este sought the glory which the encouragement of the arts could give them. Ercole, who kept a herd of exotic animals in his hunting preserve outside the city, also collected poets and grammarians. At various times Ariosto, Patrizi, Guarini, Giraldi and many lesser practitioners were received at Ferrara and enrolled on the patronage lists. On one of his visits, Bernardine was bidden to court and invited to read one of his compositions. The name of the piece is not known, but at a guess, it was a poem we have already listed as among his lost works, the *Pallas Armata,* a composition in Latin on the joining of wisdom and power, which he dedicated to Duke Ercole II.

The court was charmed by this engaging young man. He was presented to the Duke and received into the household of his son, Cardinal Luigi d'Este, Bishop of Ferrara, as Tasso was to be received fifteen years later. This favor seems to have been largely honorary, but it allowed Bernardine to wear a sword, which proved to be not a fortunate concession.

Towards the end of his law course, Bernardine had what seemed a fortunate opportunity to make use of his legal training. The Realini had become involved in a lawsuit, probably concerning the disposal of Elisabetta Realina's property. As the case dragged on for many months without being brought to trial, Francesco Realino sent his son to Ferrara to urge that the cause be given a hearing. Though, as always, Bernardine was well received in the capital city, he was unable to get the suit entered on the court's docket.

In the midst of his efforts, a letter came from his father saying that it had been decided to settle the case out of court. An arbiter had been agreed on, whose decision would be accepted by both parties. The arbiter chosen was one Giovanni Girolamo Galli, one-time professor of humanities at Carpi, and a relative of the opponent of the Realini. It was stipulated that the arbiter, before giving his decision, should ask a legal expert for an opinion on the points at issue. This part of the agreement was ignored, and Galli awarded the decision to his relatives out of hand.

Bernardine was enraged, not only at the injustice done his family but at the futility of his own efforts. But he had to contain his anger until the autumnal holidays brought him back to Carpi. One day he met the arbiter on the street, and inquired civilly enough the reason for his high-handed decision. Since the only explanation that could be given was an admission of guilt, Galli resorted to sarcasm and abusive language. It was too much for the hot blood of Realino to bear. He was engulfed by a wave of blind anger in which all he could see was Galli's sneering lips and mocking eyes. In a moment his sword was out of his sheath—the short, slim courtier's sword that had cost him a poem—and he slashed at that face.

All the anger went out of him when he saw the thin line of blood appear on Galli's forehead. Ashamed of his lack of control, still white and shaken, Bernardine sheathed his weapon and stalked away to his home. Shame kept him in seclusion for the next few days. And the memory of his deed would be a painful reproach to him for many years to come.

Though the wound was hardly more than a scratch, the affair had been too public and Professor Galli was too prominent a personage for the matter to be hushed up, even if Francesco Realino desired such a course. Bernardine was formally charged with violent assault. Cardinal Luigi and Alfonso, heir to the dukedom, interceded with Ercole II to extend clemency, but the Duke refused to stop the great impersonal wheels of justice.[2] Murder and brigandage were so terrifyingly frequent that hard, sudden punishment was the only possible course. The law that lopped off the heads of hapless Robin Hoods in the chestnut forests of Emilia must have its stern way with the young humanist of his own court. The sentence, probably given by the podestà of Carpi, was that Bernardine should have his hand cut off and pay a fine of two hundred lire.[3]

In the interval between his condemnation and the execution of the penalty, Bernardine took the course which was quite natural in the circumstances, an alternative which seems to have been at least implicit in the sentence. He fled from Carpi, returning to

[2] In a similar scrape twenty years later, Tasso was pardoned by Alfonso II. But Tasso had greater gifts than Realino to recommend him to the Duke's clemency, and he had drawn his dagger on a servant.

[3] Several versions are given of Bernardine's sentence. We follow here the one related in *Biblioteca Modenese* by Tiraboschi, who had consulted the records of the *Curia Criminale* in Carpi.

Bologna which had become a second home to him. He would be free to complete his studies in the university city which was part of the States of the Church, where the writs of the Este did not run.

It was a sad return for the young scholar whose early success and honorable reception at the Este court had promised a golden future. Yet when he counted the values that had survived the catastrophe, he found grounds for optimism. A quarrel that ended with the flash of a sword was by no means as much of a social blunder as it would be today. Indeed in some quarters it may have called out some admiration—that the handsome young bookworm had so much blood in him. Though he was barred from his home city and from Ferrara under threat of terrible mutilation, the small glory of his literary achievements was not eclipsed. He had not lost his friends at Bologna, or even among the Este. Cardinal Madruzzo was still interested in him, and the credit of a Bolognese doctorate would open many doors.

His last months at Bologna were spent in the day-long labor that had become habitual with him. His efforts were even intensified by the realization that success depended more than ever on his own endeavors. He had missed so many lectures at the beginning of the year that he was obliged to obtain a dispensation from the College of Professors before proceeding to his final examinations.

Doctoratio, the conferring of the degree of doctor, was a ceremony that once was attended with as much pomp and ritual as had been the reception of knighthood in medieval times.[4] It was one function of university administration which the Bolognese professors had never yielded up to the students' guilds. Since the granting of the doctorate was technically admission to the guild of masters, they, like all other guilds, had the right to decide who should be admitted to their ranks.

Eight years after his name was entered on the *matricula* of the *studium* as a member of the guild of arts and medicine, Bernardine was made a doctor *in utroque jure,* in canon and civil law. The entry in the university records is dated June 3, 1556, and attests: *"Examinatus, approbatus ac doctoratus fuit Dominus Bernardinus."*

[4] By decree of Charles V, doctors could claim the prerogatives of knights.

The day before, Bernardine had received his licentiate, which at Bologna meant that the student was approved for procession to the doctorate. He passed successfully the private examination, which was the real test of competence, and was ready for the formal public examination at which he would receive the doctoral title. The protocol of *doctoratio* had faded somewhat in magnificence since the days when the new laureate was inducted into the ranks of the professors by a florid ceremony in the Cathedral, presided over by the Archdeacon of Bologna. Rashdall gives some details of the procedure: the candidate escorted to the Cathedral by his promoter and his *socii*, the defense of his thesis against the objections of the professors, the proclamation intoned by the Archdeacon empowering him, in the name of the Holy Trinity and by the authority of the Holy See, to teach civil and canon law anywhere in Christendom, the investiture as a doctor and then the procession back to his lodgings, accompanied by the members of the student guilds and led by the three university pipers and the four university trumpeters. Some of this display survived, but the university records are maddeningly laconic. We know only that after Bernardine's successful encounter with the examiners (the decree of canonization notes that he won his degree *summa cum laude*) he made his doctor's oath and was invested in his new dignity. Dominus Antonio Galeazzo Malvezzi, in the name of the College of Professors, led him to the magisterial chair, handed him an open book, slipped a gold ring on his finger, placed the doctor's biretta on his head, and breathed on his neck in the kiss of peace. He was a Doctor of Both Laws. Nothing is impossible, as Chloris had said, to one in love.

Effectually banished as he was from the Este dominions, he had little choice but to remain in Bologna during the oppressive heat of the summer. He wound up his affairs and prepared to leave for Milan, for he had resolved to go to the metropolis of the north, where in the previous year Cardinal Madruzzo had been appointed governor of the duchy. He counted on his father's influence, and the Cardinal's interest in him, to find a place for him in the hierarchy of officialdom that administered Northern Italy for the Hapsburgs. Don Sigismondo d'Este, Marquis of San Martino, and his wife, Donna Giustina Trivulzio, would be travelling to Milan in the late summer. Bernardine accepted their invitation to make one of their party. Sigismondo was a second cousin of Ercole, and would later serve a brief term as Spanish viceroy of Sicily. To be in such distinguished company was sufficient safe-conduct; Bernardine would be able to pass through Este territory unmolested and even spend a few days at Carpi.

Tiraboschi declares that Don Francesco Realino was still in the service of Madruzzo at this time. But on the authority of Bernardine himself, there is no doubt that the aging master of horse was now attached to the influential Trivulzi family in Milan. Bernardine wrote to his brother in 1585:

Perhaps I shall write a letter to Lady Giustina [Trivulzio] whose kindness and that of all her illustrious house I never forget, since our beloved father's service with them was the beginning of the good things I now enjoy in holy religion. For if I had not accompanied the illustrious Don Sigismondo to Milan, God knows whether I would have had occasion to come with His Excellency, the Marquis of Pescara, to Naples, where I became acquainted with the Society, and was fortunate enough to be admitted. Praise to the Divine Majesty!

Since he had left Carpi in haste after the humiliating scene in court, it would rehabilitate his dignity in some measure to return with a doctor's ring on his hand. It would be good to see the old walled city where he was born, and the home that Elisabetta Bellentani had ruled like a queen. But the ten thousand memories of the university years conspired to make the leave-taking hard indeed. It would be only for a time, they told each other, Chloris and he, knowing how much of a trial even a short separation would be. The pain of parting gathered in his heart like a wound as the Marquis' heavy travelling carriage lumbered through the gate and down the familiar road, the cavalry escort in the red and white Este livery riding ahead.

He never saw Chloris again.

Though in later years Bernardine was to reproach himself bitterly for the time and the enthusiasm he had expended on "pagan literature," Germier points out that there is never a hint of remorse for his ardent attachment to Chloris. This is the best testimony to the purity and beauty of that friendship: it caused a Saint no regrets.

CHAPTER IV · THE CROWN OF
THE LAW

IT was a leisurely progress that the Este cavalcade made through
Emilia and Lombardy. They tarried at Carpi for a few days,
and it was evidently the last time Bernardine saw his native city.
Francesco Realino was now past middle age and his joints were
getting rather stiff for the hell-for-leather life that was his calling.
About this time he married again, a development that seems to
have won Bernardine's approval; in his letters he refers affec-
tionately to his stepmother.

On September 13th the entourage was off again, heading westward through the fertile and wooded country that lay on either
side of the Via Aemilia. It was like turning the leaves of a picture
album of Italian history. Battlefields and tombs and churches were
reminders of the surf of invasions that had poured down the
peninsula, and recalled how many lamps for the world's comfort
and enlightenment had been set aflame in Italy.

At Reggio they passed the birthplace of Ariosto and it was
only a day's canter from their main route to see the ruins of the
rock castle of Canossa, where Gregory VII had kept the Emperor
Henry IV waiting outside the walls for three winter days before
receiving him and lifting his excommunication. Almost within
spirefall of Milan, at the university city of Pavia, they would be
mildly interested to see the house where Boethius wrote *The Con-
solations of Philosophy*, and the park below the castle of the city
where Francis I had been taken prisoner in 1525. A bit of exquisite
sculpture in an ancient church, or a fragment of Greek parchment
in a dusty library was sufficient excuse for delay until Bernardine
and the Marquis had admired their fill. Or the boar hunting or
the quality of the conversation would keep the travellers longer
than they had planned at the houses of the nobility (as often as not
a cousin of the Este or an uncle-in-law).

At Pavia, it was only natural that Charles Borromeo, a young Milanese whose family was connected by marriage with the Trivulzi, should come to call on the visiting personages. Charles may have had the remote hope that the generous Este would sweeten with a few gold coins the hardship of his study of law and theology. The old Count of Arona, his father, who had a reputation for his generosity to the poor, was notoriously close with his son. Borromeo's letters to his father complained bitterly that he could not pay his creditors or his servants, or even the landlord, and that he was desperately in need of clothes.

Whatever Bernardine and Charles Borromeo talked about in that brief meeting—Greek or the law or falconry or chess—the encounter was an imperishable pleasure in Realino's memory. Years later, when he was a very old man, in a city distant almost the length of Italy, Bernardine would receive with tears of joy the news from Rome that his friend, the lawyer and ·humanist, the archbishop and cardinal, was now heaven's newest Saint.

Milan in 1556 was a prize held securely in the steel-gauntleted hands of the Hapsburgs. After a generation of brilliant warfare and cut-purse diplomacy, the struggle between France and Spain had ended with the French driven out and Charles V master of Lombardy. In spite of the stern rule and the high taxes of the Spaniards, Milan was prosperous and at peace. With one hundred thousand inhabitants it was the largest city in Lombardy, the fulcrum on which turned the lever of Spanish power in northern Italy. Its position between Madrid and the Spanish Netherlands made Milan a stronghold of the first importance in the imperial dreams-come-true of Charles V. He had conferred the duchy on his son, soon to succeed to the Spanish throne as Philip II. Philip made a triumphant visit to Milan in 1548, but except for that hasty inspection of his Lombard dominion, was content that his overlordship be exercised by a series of Spanish and Italian governors.

Cardinal Madruzzo of Trent had succeeded as governor the terrible Duke of Alba, who had been sent southward to lead the Spanish forces in the war between Spain and Pope Paul IV. The Cardinal was a choice that pleased the Milanese who would have welcomed almost anyone instead of the hard-handed Alba, and in addition Madruzzo was an Italian, and an administrator with a reputation for justice and urbane charity.

The great wheels of the Council of Trent had ground to a stop, not to be set turning again until 1562. True, the Council might have been reconvened very soon, and Madruzzo would then step back into his unenviable rôle of host to an appalling number of cardinals, bishops, theologians, heads of religious orders, ambassadors and assorted nobility. He had only one foot in Milan, therefore, and much of the influence of the paramount power was wielded by Ferdinando Francisco Davalos, Marquis of Pescara and of Vasto, with whom Bernardine would be closely associated later.

With some impatience at the dawdling pace of his journey, Bernardine rode the last few miles from Pavia to Milan on October 25th. He was presented to the Governor on November 8th. Madruzzo was impressed with the talents of the young lawyer who had dedicated his first book to him five years before. Though there was no post open at the moment, he promised that the first suitable vacancy would be offered to Bernardine. Meanwhile, the Cardinal would confer on him the rights of a citizen of Milan, which would be a preliminary to his appointment as an official, as well as a tactful remedy for Bernardine's anomalous situation as a man who had no civil rights anywhere. The decree of citizenship is dated December 12, 1556, and declares that Bernardine "because of his knowledge of law and the other considerable talents he has, will bring great credit to the city of Milan."

During the two months that Bernardine had to wait for employment, he continued to be a guest of the Marchioness' family in the vast Palazzo Trivulzi. Even in our day, the palace in the heart of the old city has been one of the places of historical interest in Milan, with its priceless paintings and sculpture, and its Dante codex as the treasure of the great library. It is highly fitting that it also has one of the copies of Bernardine's Catullan commentary.

Realino was accorded a warm welcome, and whenever he returned to Milan he stopped with the Trivulzi. Under their patronage he was received by many of the leading Milanese families.

One of the friends he made at this time was Niccolò Sfondrato, who was also a friend of Charles Borromeo, and the scion of a patrician family. Sfondrato would eventually become Bishop of Cremona and Cardinal, and then would receive the papal tiara as Gregory XIV.

As the days went by with no summons from the busy governor, the Trivulzi quietly exerted their influence. When the office of *podestà* or mayor of Felizzano fell vacant, at their instance some of the chief citizens of the town asked that Doctor Realino be appointed. Cardinal Madruzzo readily assented to the nomination. On December 12, 1556, he appointed him to the vacant post, and Bernardine lost no time packing his baggage and making his farewells to his friends. As he said good-by to his father, Don Francesco whispered to him cryptically a line from Petrarch: "Fear of disgrace and desire of honor alone . . ."

Felizzano was about seventy miles from Milan, in the territory of Monferrato. It is now included in the province of Piedmont, "Foot-of-the-mountain," which is an apt name for a plain surrounded on three sides by the Alps and the Apennines. With his cavalry escort Bernardine rode south to Pavia, then southeast to Alessandria and up the valley of the winding Panaro. It was a famous silk and wine country, and in the spring the vines and mulberry trees would march in their green ranks beside the wheat fields. Now in the winter air that made the horses steam and the roads ring like metal under their hoofs, Bernardine had no desire to delay seeing the country. He was grateful when Felizzano came in view at last, a cluster of houses on a hill that swelled gently from the plain. There were about two thousand inhabitants, a people perhaps a trifle coarse, but generous and plain-spoken.

"It crowns all the work of the law to address oneself to the governance of the State." The words of Justinian had thrilled him when he had attended his first class in civil law at Bologna. It was a small field that his powers of governance had, but it was a beginning. He was in charge, with no one to overrule him but a friendly governor in distant Milan. A great glow of contentment spread through him, as in his own house at last, and before his own fire, he kicked off his boots and stood up to warm his back at the blaze.

He was *podestà* of Felizzano for only a year, but it was an experience that would pay him dividends all his life. From the beginning he knew he was on his mettle. His reputation as a brilliant Bolognese graduate and a man of literary gifts, had preceded him. But the expression of anger that had driven him out of Carpi was known as well—and he was only twenty-six. He trod warily, weighing every decision he gave in court, bending over backwards to be just, sweetening justice often with mercy. And his absolute honesty was hardly more astonishing than his habit of dipping into his own purse to help the needy.

When his people saw the fidelity of his attendance at Mass, his recollection and manly devotion as he knelt in the Church of San Pietro, they realized what a treasure their young *podestà* was. They hoped to see him retained in office after his year's term had expired, and there seemed no difficulty in the way because the custom of restricting the chief magistrate's term to a year had been largely abandoned. But in Realino's case the strict letter of custom was observed; at the year's end he was relieved of his office. Felizzano sighed and shrugged its shoulders, and opined that young Doctor Realino could hardly have been expected to remain with them long; the great ones in Milan were probably sending him to govern some important market town.

They were amazed to find that this was not the case. Bernardine cooled his heels in Felizzano with no new appointment in sight, whether because of the opposition of a jealous few who begrudged his early success, or merely because he had been overlooked in the confusion attendant on a change of governors. For just at this time Cardinal Madruzzo had been replaced by the Duke of Sessa, a Spaniard on whom Bernardine had no claim. He was encouraged, but his prospects were made no brighter, by a testimonial letter drawn up by the towns-people of Felizzano, lauding him as "*giureconsulto grandissimo, magistrato integerrimo, uomo magnificentissimo,*" and declaring that the usual audit of the accounts of a retiring mayor had been omitted in Realino's case as an indignity to such a luminously competent magistrate.

As his efforts met with continued failure, with his patron far away and his father absent as well, Bernardine's embarrassment grew.[1] His laborious years at Modena and Bologna, Chloris' hopes for him, the swordplay in the streets of Carpi that had blotted out his prospects at Ferrara—all these memories were part of the burden that each daybreak laid on his heart. Finally an event happened that we find hard to analyze. Sore from neglect and the rebuffs of the Spanish officials, "*spe destitutus*," as he described himself—shorn of every hope—in some manner he was inspired to one final effort. This inspiration can only be described by saying that God seemed to be present to him in some extraordinary way, and a mysterious voice said to him: "Come now, shake off your depression and make your request to that royal majesty who can help those in need; and do not fear for the outcome."

Can we say that it was actually an apparition, or merely an intimation of that good counsel that Christian men find in fervent prayer? Or was it simply an hallucination induced by his overwrought state or even (for he may well have been on short rations by now) caused by an empty stomach? The question will never be solved this side of Jordan. "The royal majesty who can help those in need" was to Bernardine none but Philip II who at that time had his regal hands full trouncing the French in the Low Countries. It is a safe guess that Bernardine's desperate plea for employment never reached the King, but it came at least to the notice of Don Juan Figueroa, commandant of the citadel of Milan, who was governing the Duchy in the absence of the Duke of Sessa.

Figueroa sent him to Alessandria, a city of ten or twelve thousand, ten miles east of Felizzano. His office was that of *avvocato fiscale*, a title which is not adequately turned by "tax collector," since it included some judicial powers as well. It was an advance over his former post of *podestà* but it can hardly have been an office much to his taste. So many taxes and tolls were in force that Bernardine's humanist soul must have been wearied by the endless exactions of bridge tolls and canal tolls, tariffs on cloth and butter and hides. It seemed that Spain clipped a bit of silver

---

[1] Nothing is heard at this time of any assistance conferred by the Trivulzi. The explanation may be that their influence would be slight with a Spaniard in the governor's chair, because the Trivulzi had never been conspicuous for their loyalty to Spain.

or gold from every coin that changed hands in the market of Alessandria.

There is no record of Bernardine's activities during his tenure as *avvocato fiscale*. After two years in the custom house at Alessandria he returned to Milan. This time there was little delay before he received his new appointment. At the beginning of 1560, the Duke of Sessa sent him as *podestà* to Cassine, an unkempt little town a half day's ride south of Alessandria. To exchange the office of *avvocato fiscale* of a thriving city like Alessandria for the mayoralty of a sorry community like Cassine was a decided comedown for Bernardine. Disappointment and anger were in his heart as he rode down from Milan, through the wheat and vine country of the plains below Pavia, into the fertile uplands around Alessandria and Felizzano, and then southward into the Ligurian Apennines where Cassine lay amid the forest and mountain pastures. He followed the wriggling course of the Bormida, which doubled back on itself, raced roaring and with plumes of white water through the gorges, or flowed majestically in the larger valleys. Every mile discovered fresh views—the forest-mantled hills, the mountain torrents falling from the cliffs like torn lace, the handfuls of houses puddled in valleys.

Cassine for all its backwardness and inaccessibility might have been tolerable if it were not for the presence of an element which lay like a plague on many districts of Italy. A detachment of foreign soldiers were billeted in the town. Bernardine's biographers do not record the nationality of the troops; possibly they were Germans, more likely Spaniards.[2] Ragged and unwashed, shunted off to winter quarters in a remote mountain town when they had expected to be sent to sunny, noisy Naples, they began to live off the inhabitants with a reckless thoroughness which

[2] Burckhardt, after noting the excesses committed in the fifteenth century by Italian soldiers in conquered Italian towns, continues: "Yet outrages like these were nothing compared with the misery which was afterward brought upon Italy by foreign troops, and most of all by the Spaniards, in whom perhaps a touch of Oriental blood, perhaps a familiarity with the spectacles of the Inquisition, had unloosed the devilish element of human nature. After seeing them at work at Prato, Rome, and elsewhere it is not easy to take any interest of the higher sort in Ferdinand the Catholic and Charles V, who knew what these hordes were, and yet unchained them."

was fast desolating the country. In vain did the new *podestà*, aghast at the tide of theft and violence, protest to Milan that *"questa meschina terra"*—this wretched district, required no garrison and could not provide quarters for one. His two years in Cassine were to be the saddest of his life, and if we are looking for a "turning-point" in his career, this period is the most plausible selection.

The poverty of his people, the vandalism of the unpaid soldiers, the disappointment of his plans for a steady increase in prestige and power, the miles of mountain and plain and throbbing cities that lay between him and Chloris—all the tragic elements of his situation refuted one by one the hopes that had sustained him until now.

As the hard mountain winter wore to its end, and April unlocked the river and magicked the fields to living green again and decked the chestnut forests with their white spires, his spirits revived a little. But the spring brought the worst blow of all. Letters from Bologna carried the news that Chloris, "the lady of his heart," was dead.

Now he went down into the depths. Silent and morose, he wandered through the valleys and climbed the wooded hills, standing with a terrible temptation in his heart where the cliffs sheered off and the swift river creamed and flowered on the rocks far below. For now the futility of life was frequently in his mind and, Renaissance man as he was, he was drawn by the wrong-headed pagan valor of suicide.

That passed. He wrote poetry feverishly; again and again he saw Chloris in his dreams: once she chided him for thinking of taking his own life; once she told him she was in heaven and admonished him to order his own conduct so that heaven would be its reward. Then fever racked him, matching in his flesh the havoc grief had worked in his mind.

Only one voice could effectually call him out of his depression. Up the rutted mountain roads and across the brimming rivers of spring Francesco Realino came to see his sick boy. We can only imagine the healing joy of the reunion; Bernardine was alone no more, and with his father's arm about his shoulders he could begin the journey out of the shadows.

If he had considered resigning his position, returning to Carpi with his father and throwing himself on the mercy of the Este, he put the thought aside.[3] Though he was to remain in poverty-ridden, disorderly Cassine for more than another year, he would not seek any alternative to his stern duty. And the severe trial his soul had undergone had left him stronger, humbler, gentler. His spirituality had struck deeper foundations and henceforth he was irrevocably a man whose natural climate was prayer. He attended Mass daily, and meditated whenever the distractions of his office would permit. And, as from the beginning of his tenure in Cassine, his lean purse was open to the poor.

So passed another winter and so came another tardy, reluctant mountain spring. He had returned from Mass one summer day (it was the third of July, the day on which the Church keeps his feast), and was seated in his chamber musing on the great mercies God had shown him. A voice broke in on his thoughts, a voice saying, "Come, friend, come with me." He lifted his eyes and saw, framed in a blue cloud, a lady smiling gently at him and holding out her hand. He remained in his chair, but the lady in the cloud approached him and her hand on his arm drew him to his feet. Then she pointed to the heavens, and so the vision left him. So dazzled and consoled was Bernardine that he did something that seems to give the event an odd, even a ridiculous ending. He sat down at his table and dashed off a sonnet.

There is no doubt that Bernardine believed that he actually saw the lady in the cloud and heard her speak, although there is evidence that he identified her first as Chloris and later as the Blessed Mother. He has described his experience with such detail that it is not easy to dismiss the event with the opinion that Realino may have been deceived. Portents and visions of this sort raise a formidable problem for the biographer of a saint. It is possible, of course, to write the life of a mystic without referring to his mystical experience, but this would be to give a mutilated and dishonest portrait. In Realino's case, it would mean striking out of the record a number of events which cannot be assigned to natural causes and which increased in frequency and in their quality of

---

[3] Alfonso d'Este, who had interceded for him with Ercole II, had succeeded to the dukedom.

miracle as he grew older. It is certain that St. Bernardine was favored with supernatural perceptions of God's presence, and that later he was even given powers of knowledge and healing which operated apart from the ordinary laws of cause and effect. The cumulative weight of the evidence will permit of no weaker conclusion than this. It seems, however, that not all of the phenomena that were credited to him were genuine. When a mystic is known to be the object of supernatural manifestations, sometimes miracles are attributed to him on too slender grounds, or natural occurrences are assigned a miraculous cause. Then too, the city in which Bernardine spent most of his apostolic life lay in one of the notably superstitious corners of Europe, and it was a credulous time, when even Bellarmine believed in astrology, and popes issued briefs against witchcraft.

Yet, granted the possibility of God's decreeing exceptions to His own laws, in whose favor would He sanction such marvels if not for the saints, who are utterly captive to His love? Visions are marks of divine friendship of which a saint would hardly boast, but there are some supernatural occurrences that Bernardine admitted, to his superiors or to close associates, and more which are supported by the independent testimony of others. We shall be on safe ground if we accept these, remembering always that such phenomena are not intrinsic to sanctity, and that when a soul is proclaimed saint, the Church canonizes his virtues, and not his visions.

Bernardine's increasing preoccupation with prayer did not cloud the luster of his talents for governance. When he returned to Milan about the New Year of 1562, after completing a two-year term in Cassine, he found that he had hewn out a solid reputation as a highly competent magistrate. Without delay he was taken into the personal service of the Marquis of Pescara, who had been appointed governor of the duchy shortly after Bernardine's assignment to Cassine.

Ferdinando Francisco Davalos, Marquis of Pescara and of Vasto, was the descendant of a Spanish family which had come to Italy a hundred years before, and by prosperous marriages and staunch service in the armies of Spain had acquired enormous prestige and vast holdings in Lombardy and the Kingdom of Naples.

Vasto and Pescara, from which Davalos took his titles, were non-descript towns in the Abruzzi, on the Turk-imperilled Adriatic coast. The captain of the citadel of Pescara at this time was Giovanni de Lellis, who would have been astonished at the notion that his harebrained, spendthrift son would become St. Camillus de Lellis.

The father of the present Marquis had been one of Cardinal Madruzzo's predecessors as governor, as well as a famous cavalry general in the long wars between France and Spain. He had inherited the Marquisate of Pescara from his cousin, another Ferdinando Francisco Davalos, the brilliant *condottiere* whose arque-busiers and light horse had smashed the heavily-armed cavalry of Francis I at Pavia. Still flushed with the honors of that victory, he had died later that fateful year of 1525, after giving further proof of his loyalty to Spain. Girolamo Morone, Chancellor of Milan, had organized a plot to dislodge the Spaniards from their conquests in Northern and Southern Italy. Davalos was invited to join, and the conspirators promised him the crown of Naples. Vittoria Colonna, Marchioness of Pescara, persuaded her husband to refuse, if indeed he was ever seriously tempted; to her keen Colonna nose the whole affair stank unmistakably of the gallows.

In our own day, the Davalos name is still prominent in Spain. A latter-day Marquis of Pescara has been a manufacturer of Hispano-Suiza cars, as well as an automobile-racing enthusiast, a famous sportsman, and a crony of Alfonso XIII.

Bernardine's first assignment in the employ of this powerful family was one well calculated to test the powers of the young Doctor of the Laws. On January 7, 1562, the Marquis of Pescara appointed him *podestà* of Castelleone, which with a few neighboring villages was a hereditary possession of the Davalos family. It was a small market town thirty-three miles east of Milan on the Lombard plain. Bernardine's friend, Luca Contile, the playwright, wrote from Milan at this time to Bernardine's father:

Messer Bernardine has come to be so highly thought of here that My Lord Marquis, at the distribution of the biennial offices, found that a large number of men of substance speak favorably of him, though the greater part of them have never seen him. The community of Cassine sent to ask for him, but His Excellency wanted him for his own service,

and for the present wants him to govern Castelleone, a prosperous place
with a good climate, inhabited by some noble families, and near Cremona. My Lord Marquis paid former governors twenty-five lire [a
month], but Messer Bernardine received sixty. . . .

The spectacular increase in salary was an indication not only of
the Marquis's esteem of Realino but also of his concern with providing a magistrate of the highest competence for a town that
had become a clamorous problem. Feuds, brigandage, assassina-
tion, hold-ups, abductions went on almost unchecked. Previous
mayors of Castelleone had been too timid or too incompetent to
cope with a situation which was complicated by the immunities
claimed by the nobility and their households. A man was needed
who would be an absolutely fearless judge, with no awe for the
local gentry; who would hurry the bandits and murderers without a qualm to the galleys or the block.

We have no details of the manner in which he dispensed justice,
but it was a situation in which severity was necessary for success,
and Bernardine's administration was a triumphant success. We do
know that he heard carefully both sides of the case, and when the
issues were clear made his decision promptly; he was accustomed
to say that to prolong a trial unduly was an offense against justice
if the man was guilty, and if he was not guilty, it was an offense
against innocence. One of his strongest weapons in the pacifica-
tion of Castelleone was charity. The large salary the Marquis had
granted him was dispersed in a constant stream of gifts to the
poor and the sick. His benefactions even brought him into debt
to Giuseppe Giona, the Jewish banker in Castelleone, and to
others as well. These obligations his generous father had to meet
when Bernardine entered the Jesuits.

The trend of Bernardine's interests during these years of public
service is seen in his letters and the few other writings he had time
to complete. He was turning more and more from the goals which
his younger ambition had set, and thinking of the will of God
and his role as an object and an instrument of Divine Providence.

During one of the intervals between offices, he wrote to his
brother Giovanni Battista: "I am expecting good news from
Milan, but whatever happens, I am content with what is pleasing

to the Lord who sends it to me. I have no desire for the honors of this world but solely for the glory of God and the salvation of my soul."

And to his father, who was then ill, he wrote:

I beg you, my dear father, to receive from the hands of God, with a contented heart, the evils which afflict you, and to resign yourself entirely to His holy will. He is always seeking the good of His creatures, though this frail and miserable flesh, inclined as it is to pleasure, does not wish to acknowledge this.

The poems Bernardine wrote during this time perished completely; we know at least the names of some of his prose works, and fragments of a few of them are extant. The year he left Bologna he wrote an essay on the *De Somno et Vigilia* of Aristotle, and he seems to have sent this to his brother Giambattista. From Cassine in 1561 he sent to his brother a little treatise on the choice of a wife, in which he reminds him that virtue is more to be looked for than wealth or a pretty face, and he advises him that since he is twenty-six years old, his wife should be about twenty. If he, Bernardine, were to marry, a wife of twenty-five would be suitable for his thirty-one years. As in his earlier works, Bernardine summons a cloud of witnesses: to help Giambattista choose a wife he quotes Virgil, Petrarch, Aristotle, Plato, St. Thomas, St. Paul, Celsus, Justinian, St. Jerome and St. Gregory. Toward the end of his incumbency at Cassine he wrote a treatise on the vanities of the world, which has much the appearance of a sermon. This also is heavy with nuggets from the classics. In 1562 he wrote two essays, one on honor, the other on language, casting them in the ancient literary form of the dialogue. The disputants were Luca Contile and himself. More significant than all these for the trend of Bernardine's thoughts was a collection of notes on passages from every part of the Bible, jotted down at different times during his eight years as a magistrate.

The gratitude of the Castelleonesi for the wise rule of their young mayor was expressed in the highest terms of praise in an address from the city to the Marquis of Pescara, dated December 17, 1563, just before the close of Bernardine's two-year term:

This Catholic gentleman has proved a skilled preceptor for our city, and unwearied vigilance walked with gentleness in his care for the peace and tranquillity of each private person and the commonwealth at large. But he was resolute against crime, a wise judge, a prudent counsellor, a shrewd leader, not thirsty for gain but giving freely to the poor from his own purse. Greed's worst enemy and a powerful foe of evil, he lived honorably among us, injuring no one, giving to each his due without favor, a father to widows and orphans and others of lowly estate, for whom he was always ready to provide protection. He loved the right and put down wrong, and so bore himself throughout his tenure of office that we can say of him in all truth and fairness: Peace has come in our time, and justice restored to her place has sent forth a great light.

The letter closes, as the one from Felizzano had done, with the declaration that an audit of Bernardine's accounts was unnecessary, since he was immune from any suspicion of mismanagement.

In the absence of Pescara, who was in Spain at the court of Philip II that winter, the management of his lands in the Duchy of Milan was in the hands of his wife, Isabella Gonzaga Paleologa. Unwilling to let Bernardine go, the people of Castelleone begged the Marchioness to reappoint him for a second term. She assented, and Bernardine found himself mayor of the city again on January 28, 1564. Pescara, however, had no intention of leaving him in Castelleone any longer. On his return from Spain, the Marquis announced his intention of leaving at once for Naples. Realino would accompany him and would become superintendent of the Pescara fiefs in the Kingdom of Naples. In the event, His Lordship had to depart for the south without Realino, who was lying ill of fever at Castelleone. It was May before he was ready to travel again. He packed his baggage, wrote out notes of hand for his debts, delegated one of his secretaries to govern the city until his successor should be appointed, and then mounted his horse for the journey that would take him almost the length of Italy.

It does not take much imagination to see that day of farewell, and to ride with Bernardine through the city where the people stood cheering in the streets. The southward gate stood open like the cover of a great book, and the way led past the white haw-thorn hedges of May and the orchards where every white-mantled tree buzzed like a lax nunnery, garrulous with bees. The postcard blue of the Italian skies was mirrored in the blue of the lakes and water-courses, where the fiddle-heads and the flower-of-France grew in the weedy shallows. The hoofbeats of the cavalcade struck in trochees on the road that led Messer Bernardine out of Lombardy to Rome and Naples and Lecce, and at long last, and how gloriously, to heaven.

CHAPTER V · THE MARQUIS AND THE KING

TRAVEL in Italy of the sixteenth century was a strenuous business. The political division of the peninsula, jigsawed into twenty-odd states, fostered irresponsibility for the upkeep of roads, so that they were in worse condition now than they had been four centuries before. Twenty miles a day was good going, and the traveler might be delayed by rivers in flood, or skirmishes with brigands, or rumors of the plague that would shut the gates of cities to all strangers.

North of the Apennines, travel was more comfortable by boat on the rivers and canals that drained the level Lombard Plain. There was usually a cabin of sorts on the passenger barges, and the company was pleasant enough, by Fynes Moryson's report, ". . . so a man beware to give no offense: for otherwise the Lombards carry shirts of Male, and being armed as if they were in a Camp, are apt to revenge upon shamefull advantages. But commonly there is pleasant discourse, and the proverb saith, that the boat shall be drowned, when it carries neither Monke, nor Student, nor Curtesan . . . the passengers being for the most part of these kindes."

Realino left Castelleone at the end of May, 1564, and arrived in Naples at the end of June or the beginning of July. It was a terrible journey, *"un viaggio disastroso"* as Father Germier describes it. Bernardine had hardly given himself time to recover the strength that the fever had drained, and in spite of the brief stops he made on the six-hundred-mile journey, it was one of the most harrowing experiences of his life. He could rest a little on the river boats, but somewhere the Apennines had to be crossed, and this part of the journey would be particularly exhausting.

From his letters it seems evident that he went from Castelleone to Milan, leaving some of his baggage at the Casa Trivulzi. If he stopped at Carpi it was only for a short time and then he was on the road once more. His most convenient route now lay southward from Bologna, through the Apennines to Pistoia and Florence, but he may have gone further east on the Via Aemilia, and by boat and horse reached the Flaminian Way that drove southwest through the hills of Umbria and then due south to Rome.

Though much of Bernardine's route is conjectural, it seems almost certain that he visited Rome. Pius IV was then in the Chair of Peter, in the last months of a pontificate that would offer a sharp contrast to the stern rule of his successor, St. Pius V. The new St. Peter's was still unfinished, with the drum of the great dome of Michelangelo standing open to the sky like a samovar with the lid off. The ancient atrium still lay in front of the Basilica, as it does today at St. Paul's Outside-the-Walls. Not for another sixty years would the cleared Piazza be embraced by the lobster-claw colonnade of Bernini.

Southward from Rome Bernardine rode across the Campagna and through the Alban Hills to Velletri and on by the Pontine Marshes to Terracina. Fynes Moryson describes the danger that attended travel almost within sight of the cupolas of Rome, in the Alban Hills—where now His Holiness spends the summer at the papal palace and the lads of the North American College play baseball and swim in the pool at the old Orsini villa. Moryson writes:

And the Pope in this place gives sixty Horsemen Musqueters to accompany the Carrier . . . and to defend him from the spoyling of banished men, vulgarly called Banditi. And for this cause all passengers goe in this Carriers company, neither dare any passe alone. For these banished men lurking upon the confines of the Popes State and Kingdome of Naples, many times make excursions as farre as these mountains, to doe robberies, and the weeke last past they had killed many passengers, and had robbed the Carrier, who doth not onely beare letters, but leades many Mules loded with goods.

Realino was bone-weary by now, and after the splendor of Rome these dusty, tired towns strung along the Appian Way were a kind of anti-climax. Yet many of them had written a page in the history of Italy. St. Paul had traveled this way on his journey to Rome; the cavalry of Hannibal had thundered through, and the murderers of Cicero had passed with the severed head and hands to be nailed to the rostra in the Forum. And on more peaceful afternoons Horace and Virgil had sat under the plane trees and let the wines of the local vintages roll upon their immortal tongues.

Southern Italy presented so many contrasts to Emilia and Lombardy that, save for the resemblance in language, it might have been another continent. The climate was almost tropical and in the warm winds from the Mediterranean flourished flowers and trees that were hardly known on the Lombard plain. There were the inevitable vineyards and fields of wheat and rice, but also gray-green olive trees and palms and the exotic fruits that had lately been introduced from Mexico and the East.

Naples was like a great triangle, with two of its corners on the sea and the third in the hills upon whose sides the city had grown. The Bay of Naples is perhaps the loveliest panorama in Europe, the curving shore with its white buildings dazzling in the sun, the incredibly blue water with Vesuvius brooding over it, and the islands of Ischia and Capri just visible where the sea's blue ends and the paler blue of the sky begins.

A part of the Spanish dominions for the past sixty years, Naples had been the first conquest of that social transformation which by this time had affected all Italy. It was a transformation largely due to Spanish rule, and Burckhardt describes its chief features as a contempt for work and the passion for titles.[1] The atmosphere was headier here than in Lombardy; the extremes of blithe wealth and corrosive poverty, of sanctity and intrigue, were in closer proximity. One would become accustomed to the sedan chairs in the narrow, teeming streets, to the bright plumage of the birds that cawed and screeched in the gardens of the Viceroy, and the raucous traffic at the wharves where the galleys from Malta and Spain came in. But the tangle of racial strains that are found in every great seaport was more strikingly evident in Naples; in many of its moods it would seem to a Northerner hardly an Ital-

---

[1] Even in modern times Italy has been nobility-ridden to a surprising degree. As late as 1890, United Italy had 400 princes, 458 dukes, 985 marquises and 1679 counts.

ian city at all. The Italians still have a saying that Italy begins at
Rome.

Bernardine took lodgings in the house of another gentleman of
the Pescara employ, the cavalier Bernardine Moccia, and when he
had gotten the saddle-aches out of his muscles he presented himself to the Marquis. Though he was not Viceroy here, Davalos
was none the less a powerful personage. As hereditary Chamber-
lain of the Kingdom of Naples, he was one of the seven First Lords
of the realm, with the right to sit at the King's left hand at court
functions, with only the Grand Justiciar between him and the
royal elbow.

As superintendent of the Davalos fiefs in Campania, Bernardine
was not a royal official as he had been in Cassine and Alessandria,
but a private employee of the Marquis. Yet it was a post of vast
responsibility and with bright prospects of further honors. He had
immediate evidence of the Marquis' high estimate of his abilities
in one of his first assignments. Davalos requested him to write
from his experience as mayor a little handbook for magistrates
which would be a guide for officials in His Lordship's dominions.
Unfortunately this treatise has not come down to us. It is not
known whether Bernardine ever actually assumed his new character as deputy of the Marquis, riding from village to village to
investigate the functioning of the bureaucracy that administered
the wide Davalos lands. Events moved swiftly that summer, and
all the details have not been recorded.

One day, probably late in August, two Jesuit novices passed
him in the street. His curiosity was aroused by these grave young
men in their black cassocks and cloaks, whose silence and down-
cast eyes were witness of an inward preoccupation. When Bernardine found out who the novices were, he made a mental note
to visit the Jesuit church. His only previous contact with Jesuits
had been at Bologna, when he had once made his confession at
the church of St. Lucy to the rector of the Jesuit college. He
knew something of them by report, for Jesuit colleges had been
established at Ferrara and Modena as well as in his own university
city, when he was still in his studies.

With fresh interest, he sought more information about the or-
igin and the purposes of this new manner of religious life. The

replies, both favorable and hostile, conceded that the Jesuits were
a growing influence in Europe. The Society had been established
in Naples for twelve years, and for half of that time the Neapolitan Jesuits had constituted a separate province of the Order.
Father Alfonso Salmeron, Provincial of Naples, had been one of
the handful of scholars of the University of Paris who had met
on Montmartre on Assumption Day in 1534 and vowed to observe
poverty and chastity, and to go on pilgrimage to the Holy Land.
From that humble and almost secret beginning, the Jesuits had
grown to be a power in the Church. They were schooled by an
asceticism that opposed directly the Renaissance cult of personal
aggrandizement. Wholeheartedly devoted to the Holy See at a
time when entire nations were being drawn away from the ancient
loyalty, organized on lines which recalled the military experience
of their founder, Ignatius Loyola, the Jesuits seemed to be the
reply of Divine Providence to the prayers of the stricken Church.
"The finger of God is here!" exclaimed Paul III when the blue-
print of the Society was submitted to him, and he gave his approval in a papal bull whose opening words rang like bugles blowing the charge: *"Regimini militantis Ecclesiae."*

From the beginning the Jesuits were to be distinguished by
their adaptability, and St. Ignatius liked to think of them as a regi-
ment of spiritual militia available for service wherever the Vicar
of Christ should send them. Before long the energies of the Society
were channeled into two main streams, and these have remained
its chiefest activities: education and missions.

The labors of Jesuits in the foreign missions began when St.
Francis Xavier landed in India in 1542 to begin those incredible
journeys which would bring him to Japan and the coast of China.
Before the death of St. Ignatius in 1556, Jesuit missionaries had
gone to Morocco, the Congo and Brazil, and three had been con-
secrated bishops for a papal mission to Ethiopia. Thirty-three
Jesuit colleges were founded during Loyola's lifetime, the one at
Naples opening its doors in 1552, with a church annexed.

It was to this church, the Old Gesù, that Bernardine came
shortly after his meeting the Jesuit novices. A young priest was
in the pulpit, and Realino joined the crowd that stood listening to
the sermon. The preacher was Father Giambattista Carminata,

one of the most accomplished preachers among the Italian Jesuits, later to become Provincial of the Roman Province.

Whatever the topic of the sermon, it sent Bernardine home strangely troubled and uplifted. His trials at Cassine had committed him irrevocably to the good life in Christ, but now he felt his soul's need for a fresh orientation. He shut himself in his room away from all interruptions. Perhaps Father Carminata had spoken on the value of a general confession, because in these three days of seclusion Bernardine prepared to submit again to the keys of confession all the sins of his life.

When he felt himself ready for this act of humility he returned to the Jesuit college and asked to see Father Carminata. He entered the Jesuit's room, introduced himself and then knelt and asked the priest to hear his general confession. Bernardine's bearing and his first few words made a deep impression on the priest. Abruptly he advised him not to make his confession now. He may have foreseen that this review of a life would be a lengthy business, and he had been preparing a sermon for the following day. But he also believed that greater benefit would be had from the confession if Bernardine would occupy himself with certain meditations beforehand.

Realino agreed, and for eight days he thought prayerfully over the topics Father Carminata suggested. This was not a retreat in the full sense of the word; later, after his admission to the novitiate, he would make the complete Spiritual Exercises of St. Ignatius. In the time he could take from his work he meditated on the fundamental truths of faith, on the four last things, the malice of sin and the mercy of God. And he found fuel for the fires of his prayer in several spiritual books, among them a treatise on meditation by Venerable Luis of Grenada.

His confession filled him with a lightness and happiness which made him eager to repay the kind Christ for the prodigality of His gifts. While he was anchored in the waters of peace the thought came to him that instead of resolving to live as Christ's own man amid the honors and the distractions of the magistracy, he should make the complete sacrifice of all his hopes and his hard-merited rewards for the sake of total dedication to the service of Our Lord. The idea was, of course, preposterous, and without effort he found numerous plausible arguments against it. God can be found in any state of life, he told himself, and he took his stand on his original resolution to save his soul in the way of life he had chosen. After all, there were lawyers in heaven as well as monks.

But still the thought kept chiming in his mind. Regardless of the adjustments other men might make between the claims of heaven and the exigencies of life on earth, could he with his head-long nature and his large ambitions, keep his heart untouched by the seduction of the world? As a youngster at Modena he had found the world too much for him, and had prudently retreated. Perhaps he had been wiser at sixteen than he was now. Though he was no longer the hot-headed young barrister who had drawn his sword when the law had failed him, who could say to what excesses pride might not bring him?

Bernardine Realino was really a quite uncomplicated person; he strove to isolate the simple issues beneath every problem. His doubts resolved into the dilemma of whether he should follow the Marquis of Pescara or Christ the King, and he saw that he must choose for Christ.

Now the kingdoms of the world and all their glory made final assault. Should he abandon the career Chloris had chosen for him; for which his father had sacrificed so generously? He knew that Francesco Realino expected him to become a man of substance and influence, though his father had never pressed his own claims. Would it be disloyalty and ingratitude to his family to give up the profession which promised so much of power and property? It is difficult to appreciate at this distance the intensity of the Renaissance man's passion for fame; and it was a doubly powerful argument when it was supported by love of family. There was moreover the humiliating circumstance that he would have to ask his father to pay a number of his debts. Though he received a high salary from the Marquis he had borrowed heavily at Cassine, either because of his openhandedness to the poor or because his office demanded a rather florid style of living.

Prayer was the solvent of all his doubts, and as his resolution grew firmer, peace came and an indescribable happiness. In spite of every obstacle he would follow Christ without reserve. There remained only the question of putting this resolution into effect.

Abruptly the answer came in one of those visions that are scattered through Bernardine's life like the illuminated capitals that blossom in blue and red and gold in the pages of an ancient missal. One day in September, when he was saying the rosary, he was inundated in a surf of brilliant light, and the Blessed Mother appeared to him with the Child in her arms, and commanded him to enter the Society of Jesus. With the tender assurance that Our Lady had taken his destiny into her hands, his last misgivings vanished.

Somewhat to his surprise, the Jesuit provincial accepted him, though there was some question as to whether he should make his novitiate in Naples or at Sant' Andrea in Rome. At length Father General James Laynez directed that Realino be received as a novice at the college in Naples, and that after his novitiate he should be sent to Rome to complete his studies.

He was eager to begin the adventure, for he was close on his thirty-fourth birthday, and was anxious that not another week be wasted. It was decided that he should enter the novitiate on Friday, October 13th; and in the days that remained there was much to be done. He sent in his resignation to the Marquis of Pescara, who offered no opposition, though His Lordship's young sons, Cesare and Giovanni, attempted to dissuade Realino from a course which was making him a topic of gossip in the public houses and drawing-rooms of Naples.

With a fierce thoroughness he destroyed all his youthful writings, not because he had written anything unbecoming, but because he regretted the time he had spent in his studies of "profane literature." "It is like a net of gold," he said, "beautiful in appearance, but it ensnares our hearts." He searched for copies of his commentary on Catullus' poem, but it was quite impossible to gather them all.

At length his belongings were disposed of or packed for shipment to his family; farewells were said, and he finished the last of the package of letters he was sending to his friends and family in the North. One of these went to his brother, Giambattista, urging him to honor and comfort their father in his old age. Another, the longest and most difficult he had to write, was addressed to Francesco Realino himself. I have included the greater part of it here for the window it lets into the mind of the Saint in the most momentous decision of his life, and because the reader, having listened for five chapters to someone else's impressions, will be grateful for the sound of Bernardine Realino's own voice, human and warm and thundersweet across the centuries.

My father, loved and honored above every human thing:

I have good news for you, indeed the best kind of news. I have been withdrawn from the service of My Lord Marquis of Pescara, and have been called to serve a Lord from whose hands I hope to win in a short time joy, honor and reward without measure. Already I have given Him my word, and it causes me considerable shame that though I had been called with such urgency and so graciously, in spite of my total unworthiness, and with repeated invitations, I had refused Him my will and the poor power that is mine. It is true that this enlistment of mine may mean that we shall not see each other for some time, and this was a hard sacrifice to make, since I have a great desire to see you and to embrace you and all my family; but spurred on again and again I have resolved at last to answer the summons which so kind and powerful a Lord deigns to give me, the most unworthy of his creatures. I am quite confident that neither you nor anyone who has my well-being truly at heart could find fault with a venture like this, from which I shall reap so much profit. . . .

Until now, dear Father, in this thirty-fourth year of my life, I have lived as a friend of the world, and a friend of its pleasures, its joys, its honors and its triumphs in unceasing abundance. But at last I realize that all this is vanity, and that to one who looks closely the world itself is no other than an enemy of our salvation, an instrument of the evil one to cause us to lose our souls. Nor was this truth brought home to me by my studies in Virgil and Cicero, Petrarch and Boccaccio, Aristotle and Plato, Hippocrates and Galen, and finally in Bartoli and Baldi, with whose works I am unfortunately too well acquainted. But that true Divine Master told me, He who . . . said to me, and in a voice of infinite compassion: "Son, my dearest child, if you wish to be a friend of the world you must with all your strength be an enemy of God; and if you wish, as you ought, to be a friend of God, you must regard the world as your worst enemy." And if sometimes I answered him reverently enough: "Master, You have taught that in every situation and in every place God can be served"—there were such wonders and depths in His reply that I was forced by reason and truth to conclude with Him that for the man who wishes truly to serve the Lord of Lords, it is necessary to renounce the world, its pomps, its glories, and its joys, to deny oneself and one's own will and to choose the cross, running with stalwart step under the blood-stained but triumphant standard of our Captain and Lord Christ Jesus. . . .

Then I saw that this was impossible, or at least impossible for me, remaining, as I said, in the world; but immediately on every side there broke out new springs of water that was very sweet, though tainted, new snares of pleasure were woven for my feet, new entanglements wound about me, new flatteries allured me, new obstacles rose in my path, new desires, born always of vanity, added their weight. And all these are no otherwise than attempts to impede the good Spirit, by whom, with the aid of the divine mercy I have deliberately resolved to follow the voice of that Shepherd who well knows His own sheep since He has freely chosen them. And so I hope within a few days to be admitted, with God's help, into a flock of the most noble, most pure and most dear souls He has on earth, that is the Society of Jesus, a confraternity of priests of such a manner of life that truly they merit no other name than Society of Jesus, if indeed human merit is worth anything in God's sight. Goodness of life, holiness of doctrine, poverty of dress and riches of the spirit, ardent charity toward God and one's neighbor,—these are the things which are the joy and the constant employment of these blessed souls who are loved, honored and respected by everyone as a true image of the Church of Apostolic times. . . .

I know that human love will assert itself in you, because frankly it does in me and even while I write I feel the tender devotion of an obedient and loving son. But let us turn to our Lord and you can reflect that you do not lose a son if you give him to God, and I shall reflect that by leaving a father on earth I am gaining one in heaven. Remember that in the Old Law God commanded that every firstborn male should be offered to Him. Make your resolve, then, that you will obey God, or rather praise and thank Him without end because His love has gone before us to show us the path of obedience, delivering up His Firstborn to our service. Ah, what am I saying! Had Our Lord any need of an evil wretch like me, when He has thousands of angels to do His will? Not for His service, dear father, but for my good and for my soul's salvation has He taken me. If an earthly prince asked a father to let him take his son for a page, that would be regarded as a favor and a stroke of good fortune. Now if Christ asks a son from you, not to make him a page only, but a brother and friend, for in Scripture so He called those who serve Him sincerely, will you not give Him your son with all your heart, even kissing His feet for such great kindness?

It seems to me that you are somewhat reassured by these considerations. But with all this, my human feelings make me cry out to you: I remain indeed your son, deprived of your company, which I prize and desire so much; deprived of you, with the honor and prestige you have won, which have brought me so much joy and our family so much glory, and great renown to Carpi as well. I know, though you will not say so, that you expected me to reap some sort of harvest in wealth and property. . . . Is it not better to serve God than to serve the Marquis of Pescara, or the King, or the Emperor, or the Pope? Is it not better to aspire to high places in heaven than on earth? Is it not better to be humble with Christ than proud in the courts of princes? Is it not better to care for the soul than the body?

. . . With these and similar thoughts which the goodness of God will supply, I pray you to console yourself in the will of the Divine Majesty, that I may make your contentment the source of my own. I say the same to my mother,[2] to my brother and his wife Maria Anna, to whom may the Lord in His goodness grant children and worthy ones, to all my relatives, to all my friends, to all of Carpi where I regard everyone as my brother and my friend, since we are all members of the mystical body of Christ, which is His Holy Catholic Church, and I beg of all a prayer that the Lord will increase my faith and help me to do His will, since it has pleased Him to give me a great desire to do it. And I likewise will pray that He will give strength to such as tenderly grieve because of my conversion, that they may submit the affections of the flesh to the judgment of reason.

From here I have written many times to you, always addressing my letters to the Casa Trivulzi, since through the care of the Lady Giustina they would arrive safely; but, for whatever reason I know not, I have had no news of you in four months except for one letter from my reverend friend Fusani, written in July. I hope none the less that you are well. I do not urge you to write me, since I do not know where I shall be located, because I have not learned whether the Very Reverend Superiors will choose to keep me in Naples, or will wish to send me to Rome or someplace else. You will be informed as to the disposition of God's will for me, . . .

There remains to be said, and if it were not for the great trust that I have in you I should say it with fear, that I find that I have some debts, of which I gave a detailed account to my friend Don Niccolò when he left Milan to come to Naples with His Excellency last May, in order that if I had died my soul would not have been burdened with the guilt of defrauding anyone, nor my friends who had treated me so lib-

2 His stepmother.

erally go unrepaid. I trusted in that tender love for me which you would have poured out without stint, since whatever I have asked you have always supplied generously.

I beg you then through the love you bear me, now that it has pleased God to call me to religious life, which the laws call civil death; . . . I beg you, I say, through the love you bear me, to recover that list of debtors, if Messer Don Niccolò is in Milan or at the rectorship which keeps him so busy, and to pay them in full, especially Reverend Don Matteo Coraboni, our mutual friend, to whom I owe twenty gold scudi, for which he holds my note of hand, and the Jew in Castelleone, to whom I owe twenty-five silver scudi, for which he also holds my notes.

The other creditors are more domestic. I did not send you the account I mentioned, because thinking I would be returning to Lombardy I planned to settle these obligations myself with my own labors. I repeat my supplication that you take every possible care in this matter, nor is my insistence due to any lack of trust in that great love you have always shown me, for all that I am I owe, after God, to you. But I am driven to repeat my request by the desire of not changing my state while the world can say that I am in any way under a cloud of debt. I know that my friends will place in the father, as they have in the son, the trust that is due to our name and arms and the customs of our family.

But this is not the total sum of my indebtedness. Another creditor is Signor Giovan Vincenzo Macri, a Neapolitan gentleman and major-domo of My Lord Marquis, to whom I owe sixteen ducats, in Milanese money sixteen scudi, eleven reals. I am writing to the Illustrious Lord, Count Francesco Trivulzio, asking him to pay the said sixteen ducats to Messer Giovan Vincenzo, who will be in Milan at the end of this coming month and I will send this package of letters in the Count's care, assuring His Illustrious Lordship that you will reimburse him for every bill of mine he has paid. By the love you have for me be exact in this business, which will be a work pleasing to God also. The more I presume on you, the greater be your reward. The amount of my debts will be for a proof of the unworthiness I have shown in my public offices, though for me my conscience gives proof enough; for this whole state of affairs is due not to the Spirit of God, but, to confess what is the truth, to the human desire of acquiring glory, which is indeed an offense against God, though the world does not know it as an offense. Apart from these debts no one has any claim on me (God be praised!); on the contrary, there are some who owe me a number of scudi, but in the spirit of charity I give them all they owe me, nor do I wish that their souls be burdened with the debt on my account.

As for my effects, (or rather yours, for whatever I have I wish it to be yours), which remain in the house of the Illustrious Lady Barbara, where Messer Ottaviano of her household has the keys of the chests, as I wrote you when I left there, I do not think of anything to add. You will take charge of them for me. Please God, if it be for the best may my brother have children, who will make better use than I have of my books. And since there are many writings of mine, various in subject matter and style, for the most part badly composed and awkward, kindly do not allow others to see the works of my youth, for I do not see what good could come out of such an age, always reproached as it is by the Holy Scripture.

Signor Giovan Vincenzo will do me the courtesy of carrying by the Marquis' baggage train a trunk of mine to the lid of which will be attached a list of the things to be found inside the trunk and elsewhere; the other things that are mine I will have given away. It is certain that I shall take with me only the clothes I wear, in the manner of the apostles, in order to travel lighter. The trunk will be sent to the house of Lady Barbara.

Nothing else occurs to me except to ask you for your holy blessing, following the example of Jacob as the Scriptures narrate; may it be a powerful blessing indeed. I ask with the hope of obtaining it not for the fact that I have always loved and obeyed and honored you with all my heart; and indeed if I ever offended you (though I do not know of any instance, and never had the intention of so acting) I humbly ask pardon. I do not ask your blessing, I say, with the hope of having it as my due, but hoping that you will give it to me out of love and goodness. And at this moment I bow down, seeming to see you most ready to bless me with your heart and your hands. With this I make an end, in Our Lord to Whom be ever honor and glory, in Whom may we continue to find our joy. . . .

From Naples, Thursday, the Vigil of St. Michael the Archangel, at the twenty-third hour,[3] 1564. Your reverent son, Bernardine Realino, converted by God.

[3] An hour before sunset.

BERNARDINE REALINO entered the novitiate of the Society of Jesus on the evening of October 13, 1564, at the Jesuit college in Naples in the heart of the old city. That day he had written a final short letter to his father in which he advised him: "Be happy, since I shall be immeasurably happy"—"*Vivete allegro, che io viverò allegrissimo.*" This climate of unconquerable happiness would be about him for the rest of his life, even when the burden of his ministry was a crushing weight on his shoulders. If he had always possessed a genius for making friends, his transcendent joy would make him a Pied Piper for souls.

Novitiates by tradition are extremely happy places. Novices laugh at anything—often, and perhaps by preference, at nothing. The process of exchanging the world's standards of value for those of eternity induces a childlike spirit; the accumulated experience that makes maturity is put aside, since it has been mainly worldly experience, or rather it is reassessed in terms of the love and service of God.

At thirty-four Bernardine was older by at least a dozen years than most of his fellow novices.[1] Yet he entered as cheerfully as any of them into the round of prayer and instruction and the menial jobs which were strikingly incongruous for a doctor of the law who still wore the well-trimmed beard and the rich Spanish black of a gentleman of the Pescara house. Novices were not so segregated from the world then as they are now, and without

---

[1] Several other Jesuit saints entered the Society in response to what we would call "delayed vocations." St. Francis Borgia was 38, St. Alphonsus Rodriguez 40, St. Francis di Geronimo 27, St. Rene Goupil 35. Leaving out of account St. Ignatius and St. Francis Xavier, who were 43 and 28 respectively at the time of the Montmartre vows, the average age at which the Jesuit saints entered the Society was 24.6 years. Oldest at his entrance was the Japanese lay brother, St. James Kisai, who was 63; youngest was St. John de Britto, who was not yet 16.

doubt Realino's confrères at Naples did not find the day so minutely parceled out as do their twentieth-century brothers-in-
Christ at Florissant and Shadowbrook. But the spirit is unchanged,
the objectives identical, the methods employed the same in essen-
tials in the Society's fifth century as in its first.

We have only two anecdotes from those first days of Bernardine's life in the Society. Once when he went to the Master of
Novices, Father Gianniccolò Pedelungo, and asked for a book
which would help him to conquer sensuality, the Master replied
by pointing to the crucifix and saying, "There, read that book!"

And when Bernardine, still in his layman's clothes, was sent to
help out in the kitchen, the cook, who evidently had fostered a
latent dramatic talent among the saucepans and the spits, handed
him a rough black smock and said, "Take it, take it and put it on;
it is the wedding garment with which you will enter into the
nuptial banquet of Paradise."

Noviceship in the Society of Jesus occupies two years—the
Jesuits were the first to double the customary year. In the *Constitutiones* of the Society, which had been promulgated with papal
approval in 1558, St. Ignatius outlined the methods by which the
soul of the novice is to be orientated in the direction of the two
main objectives of religious life—personal salvation and the salvation of the neighbor. In inculcating the age-old asceticism of
the Church, the novitiate training placed paramount emphasis on
the ready obedience which Loyola wished to be the distinguish-
ing Jesuit characteristic.

The Jesuit concept of religious obedience has been more misunderstood than any other aspect of the Society's organization.
In the article entitled "Jesuits" in the ninth edition of the *Ency-
clopedia Britannica* (1890) the Rev. R. F. Littledale remarks that
the Jesuits, after all, have produced hardly any great men, and
attributes this failure to ". . . the destructive process of scooping
out the will of the Jesuit novice to replace it with that of his
superior (as a watchmaker might fit a new movement into a case),
and thereby annihilating in all instances those subtle qualities of
individuality and originality which are essential to genius." To
be sure, Canon Littledale was writing in a lighter genre than history, for more than once when he cites some instance of Jesuit

intrigue he admits that the sinister men in black, besides being devious enough to perpetrate the crime, were also able to conceal all proof of their complicity. In later editions of the *Britannica*, a more humdrum, because more objective, account of the history of the Jesuits replaces Littledale's essay—a distinct loss to lovers of the Gothic romance.

Jesuit novices in Realino's day were usually required to undergo six trials or "experiments." These were: to spend a month making the Spiritual Exercises; to work in a hospital for a month; to make a month's pilgrimage, living only on alms; to employ oneself in the humble works of the house; to teach Christian doctrine to children or the poor; to preach or, for priests, hear confessions. Any particulars of this obstacle course might be modified or omitted at the judgment of the Master of Novices, and it is likely that in deference to Bernardine's age, some of them were not required of him. But the first and most important of the experiments, the retreat, he underwent shortly after his entrance.

The month of intense reflection on the purpose of creation and the implications of man's status as God's creature, the inquiry into the nature of sin and the recollection of personal sins, the meditations on the life of Our Lord at every season from the Annunciation to the Ascension—these days, which were totally given to the commerce of the soul, were a long spiritual holiday for Bernardine. His lengthy farewell letter to his father had revealed him as an *anima naturaliter Ignatiana*, for already he had cast his spirituality in terms of service in the army of a conquering King. In the key meditation, the Call of the Temporal King, Ignatius compares Christ Our Lord to an earthly monarch who summons his subjects to march with him on crusade, and to share with him the peril and the victory. In contrast, Christ the King makes the whole world and the heart of every man His battleground: "It is My will to conquer all the world and all enemies and so enter into the glory of My Father; therefore, whoever would like to come with Me is to labor with Me, that following Me in the pain, he may also follow Me in the glory."

With all his headlong enthusiasm, Bernardine offered himself as a soldier in Christ's army. As a small boy he had paid the extravagant rites of hero-worship to his father's Lord, Rodomonte

Gonzaga. Now he gave a man's irrevocable allegiance to the gentle Warrior-King of the Church-in-arms. It was a commitment that would entail a vast outlay of energy in penance and prayer: prayer so that the soldier may know the mind of his King and His great Heart of love, penance so that all counter-claims of passion and self-seeking may be kept in check, for Christ is served perfectly only by free men.

Shortly after his completion of the Exercises, Bernardine was given the clerical cassock. He sent the news to his father in a letter written on December 12th:

I salute you in the Lord, and I send you the news that it will be two months tomorrow since I entered the Society of Jesus, and I put on the habit of a priest on St. Andrew's day, expecting that my reverend superiors intend to give me Sacred Orders [i.e., minor orders], and I think that will take place around Christmas time. And with the help of God . . . I shall never leave this Society, truly a Society of Jesus, in which I have not heard a word or seen any deed that is not for God's glory and the salvation of souls, and I know that of the fifty-five that are in the house, I am the most incompetent, the greatest sinner, the most ignorant. . . . An Order cannot be found in which there is greater charity between the members. In a word, believe me, this is paradise on earth. . . .

A letter to his brother hints that an old anxiety sometimes mars his contentment:

I do not know how to hold back the tears at the recollection of my youth that I spent in worthless employments. After Our Lord was pleased to call me into the Society, at the age of thirty-four years, I indeed changed my manner of life, and yet three things come to disturb my peace of soul: the first is that I read profane authors; the second, that I published some of my efforts; the third, that I composed some worthless poems. . . . If any manuscript notebooks of mine, in Latin or Italian, are still about the house, I beg you to throw them into the fire since they cannot be of use to anyone and can on the contrary do harm by bad example. I write these things with a vast regret and compunction for the past, ready to atone for all this frivolity in the fires of Purgatory.

Bernardine's reaction against the humanities is not an uncommon phenomenon in his century. Something similar is observed in the life of his friend St. Charles Borromeo, who, during his days at Rome as the brilliant minister of Pius IV, had gathered a coterie of humanists into an academy whose sessions were called "Vatican Nights." Later, in revulsion against his early love for the pagan classics, he had thought of replacing them with the Catechism of the Council of Trent in the schools under his control.

To be sure, the cult of humanity which the Renaissance enshrined had often degenerated into a rather noisome veneration of human flesh. Bernardine felt the necessity of repudiating the old attachment leaf and root, as perilous to the pursuit of spiritual perfection.

It is interesting to note, however, that the "profane authors" for the reading of which Bernardine expected to atone in Purgatory, were then used as texts in the new Jesuit colleges, though carefully edited when necessary. The resourceful mind of St. Ignatius had readily accepted a *modus vivendi* between religion and the Renaissance. "For ourselves," Loyola wrote in 1555, "theology would do well enough with less of Cicero and Demosthenes. But as St. Paul became all things to all men in order to save them, so the Society in its desire to give spiritual assistance seizes upon the spoils of Egypt to turn their use to God's honor and glory." And in the *Constitutiones* (Pars. IV, c. 6, E) he wrote: "In pagan books in the humanities, let nothing be read that is repugnant to virtue. The Society will be able to make use of the rest as the spoils of Egypt."

The most plausible explanation of Realino's attitude is that he regretted the motives of pride and personal aggrandizement which had inspired his literary studies and which had delayed his entrance into religion until the age of thirty-four. In his farewell letter to his father before entering the novitiate he had deprecated not only his devotion to literature but also his studies in medicine and law. There is no evidence that Bernardine as a Jesuit ever taught Latin or Greek, though he would make good use of his training in canon law as a confessor and lecturer in moral theology.

After a year of novitiate, though still remaining a novice he enrolled in philosophy classes. Somehow, the original decision of Father Laynez, that Realino should be sent to Rome for his philosophy and theology, had been changed. This was no disappointment to Bernardine; in fact when Father Pedelungo inquired about his own preference, Bernardine replied that he would prefer to make his vows as a lay brother rather than to go on for the priesthood.

The question arises what Bernardine's intentions were when he joined the Jesuits—whether he was a candidate for the priesthood or the lay brotherhood. Father Germier believes that he entered the novitiate with the goal of Holy Orders before him, but that his year of probation, with its lessons of humility and the happiness he found in menial labor, changed his mind. Though he had received minor orders early in his noviceship he cherished the desire of being allowed to serve God as the Jesuit brothers did— as porter or gardener or cellarer or cook.

If this account of Realino's intentions is true, he would not have been the first Jesuit to change goals in mid-career, or rather to choose a humbler road. Father Germier believes that Bernardine underwent this change of view, and he declares that the Saint's letters show that at the beginning of his noviceship he expected to become a priest. Yet read in their historical context the writings sustain a contrary opinion.

In a letter Bernardine would later write to his father on the occasion of his ordination he would say that he did not enter the Society with the idea of being ordained.[2] It is true that in the letter addressed to Francesco Realino on the day of his entering the novitiate Bernardine says: "I shall enter with the clothes I wear, but inside I shall be robed as a priest without further solemnity." But there is abundant evidence that all Jesuits—priests, scholastics and brothers alike—were attired as priests at that time. Until the practice was condemned in a general congregation, the lay brothers wore even the biretta, and the only difference in their dress seems to have been a shorter cassock and a shorter cloak than those worn by priests and scholastics.[3] Bernardine's statement, then,

[2] "*Son dunque sacerdote, cosa che nè voi pensaste mai, nè io certo entrai con questo animo; ma l'uomo ordina, e Dio dispone.*" (Germier, pp. 209-210).

[3] In the first, third and sixth general congregations of the Society, the subject of the lay brothers' headgear was discussed, but it was not until 1615 that the customary concession of the biretta to brothers in the European provinces was forbidden by a decree of the seventh general congregation.

that he would be *"vestito da prete"* is no evidence that he intended to be a priest.

It seems most probable that he entered the Jesuits as "indifferent," which means that he left it to the judgment of his superiors whether he would become a lay brother or prepare for Holy Orders. This decision was soon made known to him: he was to become a priest. Father Pedelungo's question elicited Bernardine's preference for the humbler status, but his own desires were sacrificed to the wishes of his superiors.

With the ready obedience which finds the will of God in the command of the superior, Bernardine began his study of philosophy. He did not mention to his professors his years of philosophical study at Bologna, and it seems odd to us, accustomed to an apparatus of credits and transcripts of "marks," that Bernardine's previous education was not already matter of record at the College in Naples. To be sure, academic programs in Italian universities were apt to be rather haphazard, and Realino may have thought that his course of philosophy, completed more than a dozen years ago, was inferior to that given by the Jesuits. But his professors were not long in discovering that Bernardine was an able metaphysician.

In his new status, half-novice, half-scholastic, he did not allow his fervor to cool. We do not know whether his poet's soul, quick to respond to every beautiful chord and color, was immoderately assailed by the clamors of the flesh. But now Mary Immaculate came to him again and set him free forever from temptations against chastity. The vision occurred as he was reciting the rosary in the chapel of a confraternity of the Blessed Sacrament which Father Salmeron had founded. Bernardine kept the event as his own secret until years later when his Provincial, Father Antonio Spinelli, asked him to give an account of the supernatural experiences of his life. At Realino's insistence Father Spinelli agreed not to mention this vision until after Bernardine's death. Spinelli died a few months before the Saint, and before his last breath he thought himself free to say that Bernardine had been liberated by the Blessed Mother from every impure thought or phantasm, and that the vision was verified by quite extraordinary circumstances.

At the end of his two years of novitiate, in the fall of 1566, Bernardine made the three simple vows of poverty, chastity and obedience and was ordered by Father Salmeron to prepare for ordination to the priesthood the following spring. This preparation consisted in learning the rubrics of the Mass, the method of reciting the Breviary, and in an effort to make holier and purer the soul that would soon receive the sacramental character of Holy Orders. He would thus be ordained at the end of his second year of philosophy, and his theological course would come later. This was not an unusual procedure in those days before elaborate and strict regulations for seminary training were invoked. Indeed, Jesuits who were not intended for the solemn profession did not attend classes in dogmatic theology but were ordained after the philosophy course and training in moral theology.

In the days that followed Pentecost, in the spring of 1567, Bernardine was ordained sub-deacon and deacon, and on May 24th, the vigil of the Feast of the Holy Trinity, he was made a priest by Mario Carafa, Archbishop of Naples. The following Thursday, the Feast of Corpus Christi, he celebrated his first Mass.

Che io viverò allegrissimo! The new wine of his joy almost burst the heart's leather on that luminous morning. These days of consecration—first vows, ordination, first Mass—seemed to lift a corner of eternity's veil and permit some dim surmise of what it is that eye hath not seen nor ear heard. None of his family had come to see him go to the altar in the radiant clothing of the sacrifice, yet he felt surrounded with all his kinsmen and all his friends. Every loved voice he knew replied as he turned and opened his arms to the whole Church at the *Orate Fratres*. With the names of John, Stephen, Mathias, Barnabas, Ignatius, with Agnes, Cecily, Perpetua, Felicity, he wove the names of his dear ones at the mementos of the living and the dead. And when the Sacrifice was over and he turned for the blessing, how lovingly he sent his *Benedicat vos omnipotens Deus* to every city and village where he had lived and loved—to Castelleone that was the beginning of his triumph, to Cassine that had been his Gethsemane, to Bologna and Modena where he had known the idyll of university life, to Carpi, "where I hold everyone as my brother and my friend."

He sent the news northward to his father in a letter of muted jubilance:

. . . On the twenty-fourth of this month, which was the vigil of the Most Holy Trinity, at the command of holy obedience I was made a priest by the Archbishop of Naples, and I said my first Mass on the Feast of the Most Holy Body of Our Lord, the vigil of which marked ten years since I received my doctorate in Bologna.[4]

Now see how great is God's mercy that though I would not have dared to desire it, much less to ask for it, He has raised me to this great dignity so that by virtue of His all-powerful words I can offer to the Eternal Father the true and real Body and Blood of the only-begotten Son for the remission of sins; an office which the angels themselves can not perform, since Christ granted it only to priests at the Last Supper. This is the greatest thing that a man can do on earth, and Holy Church has no higher manner of honoring and glorifying God than to offer this true sacrifice of the Immaculate Lamb. Certainly I am astounded when I think of my own unworthiness, but such are the wonderful works of God that He makes a just man out of a sinner, and to him whom justice would demand to be punished, He mercifully gives glory; blessed is the man who trusts in Him. . . .

I am then a priest, a thing which you never thought of for me, nor did I enter surely with this in my mind; but man proposes and God disposes. May His Majesty grant that I may be able to be His good servant, helping souls who through sin are in the slavery of the devil; for this is the object that the Society sets before it. Ardently I beg of you two things: the first, that at this good news you go before the Blessed Sacrament in a church and there give thanks to His Divine Goodness for this grace that has come to one of your sons, humbly confessing that neither you nor I merit this great gift, for that is the truth; the second, that you beg His Majesty to give me the grace to be a good servant of His, and say an Our Father and Hail Mary. If you would care to do this every day it would be a favor very appropriate for a Christian father.

Bernardine's progress was incredibly fast; the Jesuit's lengthy course of study had been telescoped for him so that he was a priest three years after he left Castelleone. To be sure, he could not give himself completely to the ministry for he was still deep in

---

[4] This is evidently an error. There is no doubt that he had received the doctorate eleven years before.

his studies. But he could occasionally go on the hunt for souls in the teeming city that lay about the Jesuit college. There was joy then in his powers as Christ's other self, sacrament-wielder, priest of the mysteries of divine love. But there was disappointment too in his own inadequacy. One night in September he wrote a poem; it was one of several he composed in those first few months of priesthood:

> You send me, Sir, so often in the day
> To tend the vines—a laggard wight like me,
> And still You know the awkward, idle way
> My hands can mar Your hopes. Oh, can it be
>
> You are content to be defrauded so?
> I cannot tell. But in Your sacrifice
> My sins are cleansed; a sinner white as snow
> I find Your blood my pardon and my prize.
>
> All that I have is largesse from a King,
> And since unworthiness has been thus blest
> Will grace go further still and make my heart
> Worthy of love, and valiant in the quest?
> Eternal Love, unwearied still Thou art
> To lead me home, and fetch the robe and ring.

News of Francesco Realino's ill health brought the presentiment of his death, for in mid-November Bernardine wrote to his father:

. . . At least for my part I rejoice that by writing I can moderate the thirst I have to be with my most honored father and to talk of heaven with him, since earth is not the Christian's home country . . . Heavenwards, dear father, heavenwards; let us leave the earth to those who want it.

It was one of the last of the Saint's letters to his soldier father, letters full of affectionate concern for his health and contentment, reflecting Bernardine's sincere interest in the doings of his family and his friends. The ties of affection for his family had never worn thin. His grief for his father's death was as profound as it had been for his mother's passing, and the ache of distance added

to his suffering. But now he was a priest, and could offer the Holy
Sacrifice for his father's soul.

He was consoled when he heard of Francesco Realino's peaceful death, and his mind's eye saw the old cavalry captain, lying
at rest after the sieges and the storming. Giambattista recorded
the death on a blank page of the Little Office of the Blessed Virgin:

In memory of how my father Francesco died on Thursday, the
twenty-fifth of December at half after the twelfth hour of night (or
rather Friday morning) with such constancy of soul and such fervor
and contrition for his sins that it would be impossible to have a more
beautiful death, and to die in a manner more Christian than he did.
Because he had the divine sacraments beforehand he surrendered his
soul to God with boundless contentment.

For all their proud waywardness the men of the Renaissance had
preserved one grace from the ages of faith: they knew how to die.

Prayer and hard work were Bernardine's medicines for grief as
they had been before, and his "joy in the Lord" at being a priest
prevailed over his sorrow. As his final year of philosophy wore to
its end the tempo of work increased; and then the possibility of a
fresh burden presented itself. Father Pedelungo was obviously failing and would soon need to be relieved of his office as Master of
Novices. Plans were also afoot to transfer the novitiate to the
Jesuit college at Nola. Father Salmeron wrote to Rome asking
that a successor to Father Pedelungo be sent. He gasped a little
at the reply of St. Francis Borgia, who had succeeded Father
Laynez in 1565 as third General: You already have an excellent,
trained Master of Novices in your midst—Father Realino.

Father Salmeron demurred, and asked the advice of his Fathers
Consultors. In his reply he pointed out that Bernardine had not
yet finished his philosophy course, that he lacked the ability and
experience to impart the religious foundation to the youngsters,
that he had no talent for discussion and speaking, a thing necessary
because of the continual exhortations to be given, and finally,
since he was somewhat advanced in years, it would be unwise to
make any delay between philosophy and theology because he
would forget his philosophy and be unable to complete the divinity
course. But once having completed his theology, he could be made

a rector in due time, for, Father Salmeron finished handsomely, "He is a prudent and virtuous man."

It seems that Father Salmeron stated the case against Bernardine in its strongest possible terms, and some of the particulars of his estimate would soon be contradicted. Borgia's decision was a compromise. Since there was no faculty of Arts at Nola, several second-year novices who had begun their philosophy at Naples would remain there under Bernardine's direction—he had already been serving as *socius* or assistant to Father Pedelungo.

As for Bernardine's opinion of his Provincial, it was undoubtedly one of wholehearted admiration, as may be gathered from two letters written early in his Jesuit life:

Our Father Provincial, Father Alfonso Salmeron, preached during this lent. He was supposed to preach the lent at Ferrara, but the Viceroy of Naples and the whole city asked the Pope for him for Naples; and so I have heard every one of his sermons. He is the most remarkable man of letters and man of the spirit that I have ever seen, and he is one of the first founders of the Society.

And in another letter:

Our Reverend Father Salmeron began last Tuesday, the Feast of SS. Simon and Jude, to lecture on the Book of Genesis in the pulpit after vespers, with a large audience of nobility and the learned. I consider it a singular grace to have entered at the time of this extraordinary Father, a magnificent pillar of Christian truth.

As matters turned out, only five novices went that year to Nola and so Father Realino became in fact Master of Novices at Naples. Father General smiled; Father Provincial sighed; the Fathers Consultors raised their shoulders and spread their hands.

FATHER REALINO was Master of Novices for two years before the leisurely transfer of the novitiate from Naples to Nola was completed. There is no conclusive evidence that he justified Father Borgia's confidence in him, though this may be safely inferred from his success in activities quite similar. To begin with, he was one of the most charming characters of his day, with an affability which novices as well as grandees found utterly disarming. We may well believe that he was deeply read in ascetical theology, for his appetite for hard work had not diminished since his university days. And what he lacked in formal training he made up by the prudence and sound judgment that were the fruit of his dealings with all classes of men as a magistrate.

He was supremely happy in his vocation, and few men have loved the Society of Jesus as ardently as he. This enthusiasm must have been infectious, for to the 'prentiss Jesuits the Master is the "pattern of the flock," the minutely observed model of the Jesuit spirit which novices make their goal. If he was as approachable as a puppy, he enforced observance of the rule with an exactness that could become graciously stern. Yet he realized that the military spirit of the Society is an ornament more of subjects than of superiors. And he was always hardest on himself.

According to the novitiate custom, at the beginning of the evening meal a few of the novices would kneel on the floor of the refectory to confess some external fault. One night Father Master joined them and accused himself of having gazed idly around the church that morning as he was sitting in his confessional. Saying his "culpa" was an act of transparent sincerity which the most cynical could not misunderstand. If Our Lady had delivered Bernardine from the power of lust, he could never say that pride was a dead dragon. Kneeling with his novices as one by one they kissed the cold tiles of the floor and declared their fault, Father

Realino was supremely the Master—the *magister*, the teacher in the school of Christ.

It seemed to be his vocation to be overworked, a condition of life that would be his almost to his last crowded hour. Perhaps he had seen his destiny and feared it when as a novice he had begged importunately to be allowed to become a lay brother. Besides sustaining an office which would ordinarily occupy a man's full day, Bernardine was attending classes in theology in the morning and afternoon. How could he feel that he was doing justice to either responsibility? Hardly would he seat himself at his table with a volume of St. Thomas or Peter the Lombard before him when a novice would come tapping at his door.

It was a relief when the last novices had left for Nola and he was Father Master no longer. But by that time new responsibilities had accumulated. In succeeding to Father Pedelungo's office he had also inherited the task of being confessor to the students of the College, and shortly after his ordination a number of the Jesuits had chosen him as their spiritual adviser—a rare tribute to one who had been in religion hardly four years.

The records of Bernardine's ministry, preserved from this period, concern mainly the young collegians who came to him for guidance. One of them, Pietro Antonio Spinelli, son of the Duke of Seminara, with Bernardine's advice entered the Society of Jesus. He became one of the most famous Jesuits of his day, a writer of spiritual books, twice Provincial of Realino's own Province of Naples and Rector of the Roman College.[1] Another was Giovanni Battista Costanzo who became a model archbishop in a day when the towering mitres rode on many an unworthy head.

One of Bernardine's clients was a wrong-headed noble urchin named Carlo Mastrilli, who attended the college with his older brother Gregorio. Carlo, who dreamed of a military career, was a reckless young hellion who caused the strait-laced Gregorio no

---

[1] This is the same Father Spinelli to whom Bernardine revealed the great apparition of Our Lady. Two Latin poems addressed to Father Spinelli are extant, evidently written on the occasion of the publication of one of Spinelli's four books on the Blessed Virgin. In one of the poems Bernardine calls Father Pietro "my soul's best part." The other contains a naive play on *spina* and *Spinelli*. Spinelli is a thorn on the branch that flowered in the Mystical Rose—a rather delicate compliment to pay to one's Provincial.

end of worry. How far along the broad highway Carlo had gone
is not recorded, but Gregorio threatened to send home Carlo's
notebook, which was full of crude sketches and caricatures. Under his older brother's scolding Carlo agreed to talk with one of
the fathers—not Father Pedelungo, because he was a saint, but
Father Realino would do. Realino's sanctity was probably less ob-
trusive.

Carlo made his confession to Father Realino and shortly afterward surprised everyone by deciding that he wanted to be a Jesuit. Gregorio joined the Society also, and in time both brothers
became highly esteemed preachers. But it was Father Carlo Mastrilli who, fifty-four years later in the hearings for Bernardine's
canonization process, testified that he owed his vocation to Father
Realino.

These were only a few of the more public instances of Bernardine's influence with youngsters. Naturally most of the work was
done in the secrecy of the confessional. Father Realino was young
enough to appreciate the great and real trials of young men. He
knew the world of wealth and honor from which many of them
came, where vice often had a social standing and religion might
be a sort of civic mechanism which engaged no cogs in one's
moral life. Bernardine blended well the chemistries of motive and
knew when to urge the civic virtues, so to say—duty, courage,
honor—when the youngster was in danger of yielding to the
powerful rhetoric of uncleanness. And he could impart his own
incandescent faith in the compassion of the Mother of God. In
temptation, he advised, make the sign of the Cross on your heart
and say: "Through your holy virginity, most pure Virgin, cleanse
my flesh. In the name of the Father and of the Son and of the
Holy Ghost."

Bernardine was occupied with his novitiate training or with his
philosophy and theology courses for about seven of the ten years
he spent in Naples. He probably was done with the classroom
not long after the spring of 1571, in the middle of his forty-first
year, for in that year Father General allowed him to make his
solemn vows of profession. Final vows are usually made only after
a long period of trial. Father Borgia cut the time to five years for
Bernardine, believing that it was unnecessary to delay the final

incorporation into the Society of so precious a subject. Bernardine made his profession on the last day of May, 1571. The previous month he had disposed of the inheritance left him by his father. (Until final vows, the religious may retain ownership of his property, though he may not enjoy its free use. Both use and ownership are renounced by the final vows.) He gave half of his legacy to the Society and half to his brother Giambattista, with the instruction that certain debts and bequests be paid. Francesco Realino must have left a considerable estate, for his will stipulated that if all his children had died before him without issue, his property was to be left to the Monte di Pietà in Carpi and the income to be used to provide dowries for Carpian young women. Furthermore a Requiem Mass was to be celebrated each year in the Church of San Niccolò, with a large alms given to the Franciscans and bread of good quality distributed to the poor.

When Bernardine was relieved of the office of Master of Novices, and then when he had finished his theological studies, he found that he had more—let us not say leisure, for that was a rare commodity in his life—but more opportunity to exercise the apostolic ministry beyond the walls of the Jesuit College. He was made a censor of books for the Archdiocese of Naples. He preached in the College Church, and gave sermon courses in the Church of the Carità to children and adults on the new Catechism of the Council of Trent. He delivered conferences to various religious communities in Naples, and was asked to preach on several solemn occasions in the Cathedral. Yet with all this, he seemed not to have been cut out for the pulpit. No doubt he lacked the histrionic parts which seem so important for an Italian popular preacher.[2] His bent was toward the personal direction of souls. This special talent was recognized when he was asked to assume the direction of a group of men, all of them of the aristocracy, who had been gathered into a confraternity by the zealous Dominican, Father Ambrogio Salvio. Bernardine succeeded Salvio when the latter was made Bishop of Nardò in 1569. Even after Bernardine had left Lecce the members continued to seek his advice by mail.

---

[2] A recent writer in *The New York Times* makes this comment on sacred eloquence in Italy: "An Italian critic, asked why there are so few great Italian actors, answered, 'They are in the pulpit.'"

He realized at this time that he was in a fair way to being taken up by the aristocracy, and to one less clear-headed it might have been a subtle temptation. The rich, after all, had souls in need of saving, and one might frequent the salons of duchesses and vice-roys without compromising one's commitment to the poverty of Christ. Indeed, a patched cassock would only endear him the more to the dramatically costumed courtiers. Bernardine had never lost contact with the Davalos family, and Isabella Gonzaga Paleologa, Marchioness of Pescara, was one of his great benefactresses. The rich he would have always with him, but now unmistakably he served notice that the poor—the unwashed, unwanted poor—had first claim upon his charity. He went to the poorest of all, the Mahometan slaves.

Slaves were a fairly common sight in Southern Europe of the sixteenth century. Some of them were Negroes transported from Africa by the monstrous treason of the slave-traders. The greater number of them were Moors taken as prisoners of war, for during most of this century Christian Europe was engaged in a hit-and-run war with the wily and appallingly cruel pirate fleets of the Saracens. Their swift ships would come from a score of ports in Northern Africa and the Balkans to raid the Spanish and Italian coasts, carrying off rich loot and slaves for the galleys and the harems.

In 1535 Charles V had captured Tunis and liberated 20,000 Christian captives, but his best prize had escaped—a terrible old man of nearly eighty, one of those Saracen admirals called Barbarossa. In the previous year Barbarossa had raided Fondi, below Rome, in an attempt to capture Giulia Gonzaga, sister of Rodomonte, as a prize for the harem of Suleiman II.

Further attempts to contain the pirate onslaughts were abortive until the fall of 1571. In that year Cyprus had been overrun and 20,000 inhabitants massacred. Venice was in terror and all Italy was shaken. At the call of Pope St. Pius V, Spain, Genoa and Venice joined the Holy See in the Christian League, with Don John of Austria, bastard of Charles V, in supreme command of the naval forces. The Christian fleets engaged the Moorish ships in the Gulf of Lepanto, on the coast of Greece, on October 7, 1571, in a momentous sea-fight which was a clear-cut victory for the League. Fifteen thousand Christian galley slaves were liberated and the peril of invasion was lifted from the West, although pirate raids still continued. For Realino, there was a sad underchord in the jubilant news of the Christian victory: the Marquis of Pescara, who would have sailed with the fleet as counsellor, had died just before the start of the expedition.

New cargoes of Moorish slaves came into the harbor of Naples with the triumphal return of Don John. Bernardine was quickly in their midst, in the slave pens and on the rowing-decks of the galleys, bringing gifts and the smiling gentleness which broke through the barrier of language. The younger captives and the sick would appeal most strongly to his compassion. Yet his converts among the slaves were few, and gained at the price of an enormous outlay of time and patience. Most often he had to content himself with the thought that Christ goes disguised in the persons of the poor.

He had become by now a personage in the city, with a reputation for sanctity that was beginning to be an embarrassment. Complicated moral questions were brought to him for settlement, and his advice was sought in the college parlor and in the confessional by all qualities and colors of humanity—the saintly and the confused, the young and the gray with sin, the stinking poor and ladies who came in gilded sedan-chairs. On all of them he lavished the sweet healing of his wisdom, dispensed with an exquisite courtesy that recalled the blond young humanist of the Este court. But now the fires of prayer had burned away the vanity and personal ambition. Is it any wonder that some, in whom piety had mated with acquisitiveness, snipped off pieces of his cloak or the ends of his cincture for relics? This petty persecution of the devout would follow him all his life.

His fame at Carpi as the hot-headed young swordsman was enlarged by the news from Naples that the brilliant lawyer turned Jesuit was being hailed as one of the most influential priests in the Regno. The establishment of a Jesuit college at Carpi was being discussed, and the townspeople were enthusiastic for Bernardine's return as rector of the new foundation. He smilingly shrugged off the suggestion, while favoring the founding of the school. But at his brother's request he did ask leave to make the journey to Carpi after Giambattista had seen two of his children carried off by sickness. That was in 1570, when Bernardine was fairly launched on his career as a director of souls, and Giambattista had become, it appears, a physician. Bernardine's superiors decided against the long trip back to Carpi, since there were so many employments that required his presence in Naples.

In one of his letters to Giambattista he says:

I began this letter yesterday morning, and I must have sat down to it forty-six times, and I did not finish it until this morning, which is the feast of the Purification of the Madonna, there were so many things to keep me busy—being called here and there to hear confessions or for other works of charity in the house or outside. But God be praised Who gives us the strength. . . .

The next four years were all of one pattern—preaching, counselling, visiting the slaves and the sick, and ever more increasingly listening to the files of penitents that queued up at his confessional. He saw that hearing confessions was to be his special apostolate, and he realized that it would be a kind of crucifixion. He had a pronounced dislike for the work of the confessional.

The Neapolitan chapter in his life came to an abrupt end in December of 1574 when he was assigned to Lecce, at the opposite side of the peninsula. Father General Mercurian, at the request of the civil authorities in Lecce, was sending two Jesuit priests with a view to opening a Jesuit house in the city. Father Realino would be accompanied by a lay brother named Alfonso, and a Father Giacomo Abate would join them in Lecce.

Father Bernardine's friends and clients were indignant at his removal, and Father Salmeron was grateful that he could shrug his shoulders and gesture expressively in the direction of Rome. They were welcome to send their remonstrances to His Paternity if they would. But meanwhile Father Realino's day of departure had come, and he had packed his luggage and quietly made his farewells and had ridden off in the *diligenza* with Brother Alfonso.

The road lay through the Neapolitan Apennines to the plain of Capitanata on the Adriatic coast, and then southeast through Bari and Brindisi along the coastal highway. After a week in the jolting *diligenza*, through the mountain cold and over the indifferent roads of Apulia, the travelers were dog-tired when they came within sight of Lecce.

On the great cavalry boot of the Italian peninsula Naples lies at the western edge, a little above the instep, where the strap of a spur would cross, and Lecce a little below the middle of the high heel. This heel-of-the-boot peninsula is a country of rolling moorlands and pasturage, of wheat fields and stone-green olive groves, ringed with little sea cities whose modern names are corruptions of famous ones in the history of Magna Graecia and the ancient wars of Rome. Lecce is midway between Brindisi and Otranto, seven and a half miles from the Adriatic, in the section called Terra d'Otranto.

Lecce has laid little claim to public notice in the past few centuries, except perhaps for the cheap papier-mâché statuary it produces, or the snuff of which Napoleon was fond. The city's buildings, from the remains of a Roman amphitheater in the Piazza Sant' Oronzo to the palaces and churches in the sixteenth-century baroque, are monuments of the halcyon days before history packed up and left this corner of Italy. It was a thriving municipal town under the Romans, and in medieval times as well, when the cities of Apulia were bridgeheads for the trade with the East. The successive tides of invasion that have broken over Southern Italy washed through Lecce—Goth and Greek and Saracen and Lombard and Norman. The Norman Tancred, fifth Count of Lecce and later King of Naples, brought the Cluniac monks to Lecce in the twelfth century and built them the lovely Church of Santi Nicola e Cataldo which still stands outside the city amid the flowers and the cypresses of the Campo Santo.[3] The quietly beautiful doorway, outlined in bands of carving as delicate as figured damask, is in sharp contrast to the cymbal-clash splendor of the baroque. For Lecce is a baroque city, full of palaces and churches worked in that much maligned idiom from the golden stone of the region. Paul Bourget, the French critic, in his *Sensations d'Italie*, found the opulence of Leccean baroque tempered with "an in-

---

[3] Cataldo was of course St. Cathal, a seventh-century Irish bishop from the County Waterford who was shipwrecked at Taranto on his way home from Jerusalem. His miracles and preaching reformed the city, which thereafter cherished him as its patron saint.

describable delicacy" which he credited to Hellenic influence. This mixture of racial motives in the Lecce architecture is most palpable in Tancred's church, for the piers are Romanesque, the narrow nave and the high vaulting are Norman, but there are Moorish lines in the haunches of the pointed arches, and the great dome over the crossing is Byzantine.

Half the nations of the West had flown their flags from the ramparts of Lecce when Charles V, worried by the never-ending menace of the marauding Turks, sent his engineers in 1539 to fence the city with new ramparts and watchtowers and a wider foss.

There was a population of 30,000 in this busy outpost of Christendom when Bernardine came through the chilly mountains and across the milder plain, past the villages where the dialect was more Greek than Italian, along the provincial highroad that brought him at last within sight of the walls and belfries of Lecce.

It was the German historian Ferdinand Gregorovius who called Lecce "the Florence of Apulia"—in a book which acquired the raffish distinction of being listed on the Roman Index. It is a comparison which has been justified down to our own time. "Undoubtedly one of the most charming and beautiful towns in Southern Italy," a modern writer says of Lecce, "for not only is it full of interesting churches and works of art, but in its intelligence, civilization, and hospitality it resembles that fairest city on the Arno. . . ." [4]

One of the earliest humanistic academies in Italy had flourished at Lecce and the city had begotten poets and painters of its own. Yet, for all that, Apulia was remote hinterland, and though conditions were certainly better in the towns, the province was known for its ignorance of religion and general backwardness. The early Italian Jesuits applied the phrase "the Italian Indies" to Apulia as well as to Calabria and the Abruzzi, the wild Italian Ozarks east of Rome.

Bernardine was soon to realize what a fool's parliament of political bickering had preceded his coming. The rivalry between bourgeoisie and nobility, so frequently met with in medieval history, had taken a comic opera turn in Lecce. In 1542 a decree of Charles V had provided that the nobility and the bourgeoisie should govern the city in alternate years. This mandate was im-

[4] Edward Hutton, *Naples and Southern Italy*, New York, 1924, p. 224.

perfectly observed, for the records indicate that for the next half-century commoners occupied the mayor's chair only in one year out of three. When the commoners came into power in 1573 there, was a wholesale tearing up of the edicts of the preceding adminis-tration. The city council canceled the negotiations which the nobles had set on foot to bring the Jesuits to Lecce, and in a fine fervor of anti-nobility enthusiasm, forbade the members of the Society ever to take up residence in the city. It was a regulation which no one ever took seriously, and Father Salmeron sent Father Mario Fabritiis to preach in the city in the fall of 1573. He remained until Easter of 1574 and labored with wonderful success. In 1574, when the nobles may have been again in power, the act banning the Jesuits was revoked and a fresh petition was sent to Salmeron; three thousand gold scudi had already been subscribed for a proposed Jesuit house.

If Father Realino feared that his coming would reopen the old feud, his welcome reassured him. A mile outside the city a troupe of horsemen met the travel-spattered *diligenza* and as the coach-man pulled the post ponies to a stop and flourished his hat, the leader of the cavalcade dismounted and himself opened the door and bowed the startled Jesuit out of the carriage. Arrayed along the roadside were the leaders of the government and the nobility, sitting their horses as proudly as the Pope's nephews, tastefully overdressed in the baroque magnificence of plumes and buckles and cloaks. For a moment Bernardine wondered whether it was one of those elaborate practical jokes that the idle nobility so much admired—but surely they would not make a fool of a priest. There was a mount provided for him, and though it was a long time since he had had thoroughbred horseflesh under him, he tucked up his cassock and went into the saddle in a style his cavalryman father would have approved.

The procession clattered off down the level highway, through the Arch of Charles V which the canny Lecceans had made out of one of the gates of the town, and then through the crowded streets. Everywhere there were people applauding, and Bernardine bowed and lifted his hat and smiled and smiled until the joy and the clamorous welcome of his first hour in Lecce quite over-mastered him, and even a man much more phlegmatic than he would have been hard put to restrain the tears at such a time. The distinguished escort left him finally at the house of Baldassare Catalano, where he would be a guest for the time being.

The next day, Father Realino's first concern was to pay his respects to the Vicar Capitular, for the Bishop of Lecce was absent. Then he celebrated Mass in the Cathedral, and in a modest little address to the Canons he said that he had come to the city only to be of service, and that they must not spare him. For forty-two years Lecce took him at his word.

CHAPTER VIII · LETTERS FROM
LECCE

O̶ur Lord be ever praised!" Bernardine wrote to Salmeron three days after his arrival. "On Sunday at the twenty-second hour we arrived in this noble, pious and cultured city of Lecce, hale and hearty, though there were many inconveniences inseparable from a long journey. We were received with such enthusiasm by all the chief men of the city that I was bewildered, as I am each day, at their great hospitality and the kindness they show us. I will not go into details. . . . It is sufficient that Your Reverence understand how great are the affection and devotion that the city shows on all sides to Ours. . . ."

Bernardine continued that he had been surprised at the size, wealth and culture of Lecce. He thought it would be a fine location for a Jesuit college, and there was some sentiment for it in the city.

He plunged at once into the work of the ministry. Immediately after his first Mass at the Cathedral, he visited one of the city's two prisons and in the evening he began in the Cathedral pulpit the course of doctrinal instructions that he would continue on feast days. Meanwhile Father Abate joined him and they divided the work between them, Father Abate preaching in the Cathedral on Sunday mornings and Bernardine in the evening. In addition, Bernardine taught catechism to the children on Tuesdays and Thursdays, gave conferences in convents and monasteries, and visited the sick and dying.

The month after their arrival, the Jesuits were given the little Church of the Annunziata, which soon proved to be too small for the crowds that came to Mass and confession. For in a short time Father Realino began to exercise a large spiritual influence on the city and it is a happy duty to record that the diocesan authorities and the other religious orders in Lecce were wholehearted in their support of the newcomers. Among their friends were the prior of the Dominicans, who generously praised Bernardine from the pulpit of the Dominican church, and lauded his sermon courses and his teaching of catechism.

The temporary quarters provided by the city were more than satisfactory. Bernardine wrote to Salmeron:

The food is abundant and of good quality and well-prepared; and as for the wine, I do not think that Your Reverence has ever tasted anything so delicious or so good for the stomach. The city provides for us, but individuals are always doing us favors, which I am accepting. We have two rooms with three beds—very good ones with two mattresses each and three blankets, and each mattress would make two of the ones we are accustomed to. . . .

The matter of providing a residence for the Jesuits and a large church was not allowed to drift. The Lecceans who had sponsored their coming set about giving practical form to their plans. There was growing support for the idea of building a college in Lecce, and the proposal that the city undertake to finance such an institution was debated in the city council. The councillors were overwhelmingly against the measure. The municipality was in debt, and there seems to have been vigorous opposition also on the score of free tuition. It was a reaction that Jesuits had met elsewhere: schoolmasters who lived on their tuition fees were naturally suspicious of the new schools which educated gratis. But the council sent off a letter to Father Mercurian asking him to allow the foundation of a professed house. Mercurian agreed, stipulating, however, that the house and a church must be permanently assigned to the Jesuits.

A professed house, as distinct from a novitiate or a house of studies for Jesuit scholastics, or a college for lay students, was a residence for those professed of final vows who devoted themselves to the spiritual ministries of the Society. These residences, like the churches to which they were attached, could have no funded revenues, even for the upkeep of the building or for vestments or altar supplies. They depended on the Providence of God and the day-to-day charity of the faithful.

The Lecceans acted without delay. Before six weeks had elapsed, four gentlemen had taken title to a mansion in the heart of the city, the former home of a royal official, with the view of presenting it to the Society as a professed house. Two smaller buildings were also on the property, and an adjacent garden, the property of the Vicar Capitular, was also to be given to the Jesuits. Bernardine jubilantly announced the gift in a letter to Salmeron, sending him a list of the principal donors and a copy of the deed, drawn in the names of the four sponsors, Scipione Bozi, Cesare Prioli, Giantommaso Giaconia and Luigi Fedele.

Salmeron was astounded at this sudden development and wrote to Father General Mercurian that Bernardine had far exceeded his instructions, which were to survey the prospects for a Jesuit foundation and to act only on decisions made by his superiors. Bernardine had not helped his own case, because in a letter he wrote to the General announcing the gift of property he had asked that the celebrated Father Giovanni de Rosis, a Jesuit architect, be sent to Lecce to survey the site and draw plans for the church. Father Mercurian might rightly have concluded that matters were moving too hastily in Lecce. He accepted Salmeron's indignant account of Father Realino's activities, and he instructed the Provincial to give him such admonitions as he thought suitable.

In his reply to Salmeron, Bernardine assured him that he had never considered himself anything but an instrument of the Society. He had not assented to any purchase; he had explicitly informed the Leccean benefactors that he had no power to accept the property. His position was quite clear, and the gentlemen had acted independently. If Father General should decline their offer, the house could be sold at any time, and at a considerable profit, and with no scandal resulting, since the Society had not been involved in the purchase. The legal papers had been sent only for the sake of giving information; the Society would have no right to the property until a formal donation had been made.

But Salmeron was not won over. In forwarding to the General some letters Bernardine had dispatched through Naples, Salmeron wrote to Mercurian:

Father Bernardine Realino sends the enclosed letters, from which Your Reverence can see what sort of defence and excuse he offers for the error committed. He wrote me a long letter in which the more he discusses this business and makes excuses for it, the more he involves himself and shows his own culpability. . . . If I did not know the great goodness and virtue of this Father, I would say that though it is human to err, yet not to recognize the error is a diabolical fault—from which of course this Father is far removed, since he is entirely good and so innocent that the Lecceans have used him for their own advantage.

The plans of the property which Bernardine sent to Rome so impressed the General and Father de Rosis that Mercurian wrote to Bernardine and to the Leccean benefactors giving his approval for the acceptance of the property. In the same post came a letter from Father Salmeron insisting that a contract be drawn up in legal form and that only then could the donation be accepted. There was some confusion over the independent letters, and some indignation on the part of the Lecceans, who protested that they were men of their word and would go through with their undertakings. Father Salmeron reported to the General that the Society was laying itself open to being swindled—by four generous if somewhat weary gentlemen who were doing their gracious best to persuade the Jesuits to accept a princely gift.

Father Mercurian brought the pettifogging to a halt by standing by his promise that Lecce would have a professed house. It would be inappropriate to exact a written contract, since the transaction was one of sheer charity, and not financed by the municipality. And if the Jesuits insisted on a contract, the Lecceans on their part might require written guarantees as to the number of Jesuits to be assigned to Lecce.

The architect de Rosis was unable to come to Lecce because of the new constructions that kept him occupied in Naples and Rome, but the plans he drew according to Bernardine's specifications were used in the construction of the church. Father Salmeron informed Bernardine, in a letter whose ink fairly sputtered on the page, that he could expect no Jesuit reinforcements from Naples, since the rookeries he had acquired did not merit them. And far from sending the distinguished architect, they would not send him even a single housepainter.

So ended an episode which, if it does not add to the stature of Father Salmeron, at least dislodges him not at all from his secure place in history as one of the first companions of St. Ignatius and the theologian who, at thirty-one, was a compelling spokesman for orthodoxy at the Council of Trent. Possibly Bernardine was at fault in not remembering the detonating temperament of his superior; certainly the affair is a tribute to the calmness and statesmanship of Father Everard Mercurian.

It was in February, 1575, that the Jesuits finally accepted the magnificent donation of their Leccean benefactors, and in September the work of demolishing the smaller buildings on the site was begun. The mansion was evidently to be used as the residence of the fathers. Bernardine's encounter with Father Salmeron may have made him wary of too much haste; and another reason for the delay was a dispute with certain Greek Catholics in the city. Adjacent to the acquired property was the Church of San Niccolò dei Greci, which served a Greek Catholic parish. The plans for the Jesuit church would either carry the transept onto the area occupied by the Greek church, or would bring the two edifices into impossibly close quarters. Monsignor Cesare Busdrago, Bishop of Alessano, the ordinary of the Greeks, wished to allow the church and an adjoining small house to be demolished and to transfer the land to the Jesuits, with the Greeks being given in exchange the larger and more handsome Church of San Giorgio. The Greek Catholics flatly refused the offer and the dispute which ensued was carried on so hotly that eventually it had to be referred to the Holy See for a decision.[1]

The reluctance of the parishioners to abandon their familiar parish church is readily understandable, in the context of the history of the Oriental rites in Italy. Time out of mind there had been numerous Greek Catholic churches in southern Italy, with their own bishops and several monasteries. After the Norman invasion the Greek dioceses were suppressed and the Greek clergy and people were made subjects of the Latin bishops. There is no doubt that the Greeks were exposed to considerable pressure, and

[1] An interesting, if inaccurate version of this incident is given in Brigg's *In the Heel of Italy*. "Perhaps the most striking event of sixteenth-century church history in Lecce was the arrival of the Jesuits in 1574, a small body led by Father Bernardino Realino da Campi [sic]. Content to begin in a small way at Lecce, they drove out the Greeks from the church which the latter occupied, commenced to hold their own services there, and speedily created a party in their favor in the city."

even some force, to induce them to adopt the Latin rite. The Apostolic Constitution *Etsi Pastoralis* of Benedict XIV in 1742 forbade any further hostility to the Greek rites, and approved the practice of the Byzantine liturgy, while leaving priests and people subject to the Latin hierarchy.

The parishioners of San Niccolò dei Greci resisted what they thought was another invasion of their rights and it may be that the Latin Ordinary and the Jesuits carried matters with too high a hand, and with too little consideration for the Greeks' attachment to their parish church. The case dragged on with Rome's proverbial slowness, but eventually Gregory XIII decided against the Greeks.

Meanwhile the first stone of the new church was set in place on September 21, 1575, and the work went quickly forward. The yellow stone came in from the quarries, in the low-slung stone drays, drawn by the deliberate oxen. Bernardine was at the site as often as the growing demands of the ministry would allow. He would go prowling through the forest of scaffolding, seeing in the raw walls and the shored-up arches the shapes of soaring space that the architect's baroque imagination had planned. He complimented the workmen generously and, when he could, gently urged them to a better observance of their religious obligations. A great tide of exaltation was rising in his heart as the walls grew and the stagings were knocked down and the vaults stood high and free.

About this time he had come to live in one of the houses on the property—probably not the mansion, for he admitted to Mercurian that it was like living in an open field. Frequently Bernardine and Brother Alfonso were alone, because Father Abate had relatives somewhere in the province and sometimes absented himself on family business. Now that they were out of their hired lodgings, the problem of meals became quite grave. Brother Alfonso seems to have been of little help, and when Father Abate was allowed to take the Brother with him for a companion Bernardine hired a servant. He was a bricklayer who was sincerely devoted to the Jesuits but turned out to be a resounding failure in the kitchen. Father Realino was quite willing to get along on the food which kind neighbors were always sending in, but under the remonstrances of his friends he hired another servant to succeed the bricklayer.

This man turned out to be worthless, a scoundrel who gradually extended the scope of his laziness and dishonesty as he perceived the meekness and patience of his employer. He appropriated the best food for his own use, and often left Father Realino to go hungry. His easy familiarity must have been as repulsive to the Saint as his occasional eruptions of coarse abuse.

Bernardine became sick in the summertime, and though he kept on his feet through the intense heat of August, on the last day of the month he had to take to his bed. For three weeks he sweated and ached and tossed with fever, unable to touch food or to sleep except in brief fitful flights. He was convalescent in September and back at his accustomed round of sermons and visits and confessions the following month.

During this time, one of the doctors who came to see him prescribed white wine to help him recover his strength. There was no white wine in the house, but a kind neighbor, Porzia Ventura, undertook to provide it. The first pitcher of wine came with the message from Signora Ventura that she had just emptied one wine barrel, and that she would broach another the following day and the wine would be of better quality. Father Realino sent his thanks and his compliments for the quality of the wine and added somewhat cryptically that there was no need to open the second barrel, but to continue drawing the wine off from the first. The lady thought that Father Realino must have misunderstood her message, but the following day the supposedly empty barrel yielded another pitcher of wine, as it continued to do for some weeks, until Father Realino sent word that he had no further need for the wine.

Though this marvel does not seem as well authenticated as some of Bernardine's later prodigies, it would be appropriate if his beginning of miracles in Lecce was an increase in the quantity of wine—an echo of the Cana courtesy of his Master.

This siege of fever may have been one of the occasions—there were at least two of them during his first years at Lecce—when illness coincided with attempts to remove Father Realino. In March of 1576 Father Claudio Acquaviva became Provincial of

Naples, bringing to a close Father Salmeron's administration which had begun in 1558. Acquaviva was later to command the entire Society of Jesus for thirty-four years as one of its most able generals. In the year of his accession to the governance of the Neapolitan Province, he informed Father Realino that he was about to recall him to the scene of his first apostolic labors. Bernardine prepared to leave Lecce, but the fever caught him in the midst of his final arrangements for departure. He was not strong enough to travel until autumn, which turned out to be a rather stormy season. Father Provincial was reluctant to allow Realino to make the tedious journey through the mountains, with the rain falling steadily; his return to Naples was postponed.

Acquaviva came to Lecce himself in the following spring, and though he had expected to stay one week, stayed a fortnight longer. He preached twice in the Cathedral with general satisfaction and was urged to stay all the spring—an invitation which it must have been a hardship to refuse, for the fair, fresh weather and the flower-brimmed towns made spring in Apulia a strong enchantment indeed. The Provincial was evidently satisfied that Bernardine's proper niche was in Lecce, for he gave up his attempt to recall him. But three years later, in 1579, Father General Mercurian wrote that Bernardine should prepare to come to Rome to assume the rectorship of the professed house which was the headquarters of the Society of Jesus and the residence of the General. Again sickness interfered, and though Mercurian's order still waited on his recovery, before he could gather enough strength for the journey, the General changed his mind.

When the new Jesuit church opened its doors it had been two years under construction and was not yet completed. Because of the litigation with the Greeks the transept was unfinished and the airy dome that de Rosis had planned for the crossing of the nave and the transept was still lacking because of a shortage of materials and of funds. A wooden roof over the crossing would suffice for the present. But the apse and the nave were otherwise completed, and since the Annunziata was so hopelessly small, there was every reason for opening the larger edifice.

The church was dedicated to the Most Holy Name of Jesus, and so would be familiarly called Il Gesù as were the principal churches of the Jesuits in Naples and Rome. It was in the florid baroque which attempted a freer, non-academic translation of the forms of imperial Roman architecture. At its best, baroque merely substituted a newer and fresher classicism for the old. At its worst, the style often seemed to be the creation of pastry cooks rather than architects. The Jesuits' use of untrammeled baroque in their new churches in Italy gave rise to the term "Jesuit style," a term not usually employed as a compliment.

The peril of the baroque was the hazard that always besets the romantic imagination: the need for an exact understanding of the measure at which ordered abundance becomes surfeit. The classical motives of column and architrave, round arch and barrel vault were employed, but were subjected to a sovereign passion for ornament. Arches were broken and lines were intricately curved, sculptural rosettes and modillions, swelling shields and scrolls and brackets overflowed the pediments and cluttered the clean classical lines of lintel and column; and the columns were rusticated or twined with sculptured laurel or twisted out of shape, like the wriggling pillars of bronze that support the *baldachino* in St. Peter's.

Compared to the splendor of polychromatic marble, metal sunbursts, and sculptured figures thronging out of the broken pediments, which distinguished Sant' Ignazio and the Gesù in Rome, the Lecce Gesù is rather plain. A wide, unobstructed nave lighted by clerestory windows ends in a deep apse; Ionic pilasters support an Ionic entablature, with round arches between, framing the four chapels on either side of the nave; and there are grouped Ionic pilasters at the four piers supporting the crossing. The pilasters and faces of the arches are coffered simply and at the clerestory level not ornamented at all. The makeshift timber ceiling over the crossing would later be replaced with a painting by the Jesuit brother, Andrea Pozzo, whose mastery of depth and distance is best exemplified in his masterpiece, the ceiling of Sant' Ignazio in Rome.

It is in the apse and the side chapels that the Lecce Gesù vindicates its title as a baroque church. The generosity of private donors and the luxurious taste of the decorators have surrounded the altars with all the *brouhaha* of erupting pediments, cluttered columns, superimposed niches and sculptured hearts and flowers. Yet a certain grace and dignity are never lost. The clean, hard lines of the architect's design saved the Gesù from vulgarity; appropriately for the exquisite restraint and temperance of Bernardine's humanist heart, his church is *allegro ma non troppo*.

The Gesù was opened to the public on Sunday, October 25, 1577, and in the evening Bernardine started a course of sermons on the Book of Genesis, and another Jesuit, Father Giulio Turi, began to teach Christian doctrine. There were now five Jesuits in Lecce: Father Turi had been recently sent there by the Provincial, with a lay brother to be sacristan of the church, and Father Abate and his companion, Brother Alfonso, seem to have returned.

The conviction Bernardine had formed on his arrival in Lecce, that the city was an apt location for a Jesuit college, was widely shared. In spite of the initial setback in the city council, a number of families were determined that the college would be founded even if it had to be financed by private donations, as the church had been. A wealthy patrician, Raffaele Staivano, pledged an annual donation of a thousand ducats, and other gifts quickly followed. The generous Lecceans, who had just built a magnificent edifice for the Jesuits, and who during two decades would build four other churches in the city, gallantly dipped into their purses again. Some were fathers of families who wanted their sons educated in one of the new schools. Others gave with no thought of personal advantage but out of pure loyalty to the Catholic faith, or in gratitude for the tireless charity of Father Realino. And though the municipality of Lecce could not see its way clear to financing a college, a number of small towns in the vicinity pledged an annual contribution.

The college building rose more promptly than the church, so promptly, in fact, that the stone masons declared that the walls were measurably higher in the morning than when they had left them the previous night—a marvel immediately ascribed to the prayers of Father Realino.

An imposing three-story building with broad corridors and large rooms, the college on the exterior has some of the majestic grace of the Renaissance town houses in Florence and Rome. Two rows of superimposed Corinthian pilasters support cornices dividing the façade into two planes; between the pilasters the windows are capped with handsome pediments. Yet though there is no ornamental extravagance, the building lacks the authority and unity of design of the church.

Begun in 1579, the college building appears to have welcomed its first classes in the autumn of the following year. In June of 1580 Bernardine wrote to his brother, exhorting him to work for the foundation of a Jesuit college in his home city:

> May it be the will of our sweet Jesus that Carpi open its eyes and take steps to have a college founded, and you ought to begin the work with a vigorous effort, for even if there are difficulties at the start, God's business always carries off the victory. I have seen it here where already this college was enriched by a thousand ducats at the beginning of the year by a young man who is my penitent—and a holy man he is—and other large bequests and gifts so that a handsome church stands equipped with costly furnishings and a stately house surrounded by the affection which binds the city to the Society. We shall not fail to feed them with spiritual food: Christian doctrine, sermons, lectures on feast days, confessions, communions, solutions of problems of conscience, and assistance to prisoners at death. The classes in humanities will begin in September, and then by degrees those in philosophy and theology.

It is somewhat surprising to find that the solemn inauguration of the college did not occur until three years later, on September 25, 1583. Since the school was certainly a going concern long before that, we may surmise that the ceremonies coincided with the institution of the lectures in philosophy, so that, in our terminology, the preparatory school became a college in fact. There had been a corresponding increase in the Jesuit personnel, and on the occasion of the inauguration of the college, one of the newcomers, Father Giannicolò Petrella, was named the first rector. Presumably, up to that time Bernardine had governed the community as Superior; with the institution of a college faculty the head of the community would be of higher rank.

We must not readily suppose that Father Realino had been passed over in cavalier fashion and humiliated in the house he had founded. It was natural that the rector of a faculty of arts should be a man with abundant classroom experience; Bernardine had devoted himself exclusively to the spiritual rather than the educational ministry.

Even so, he would later serve a term as rector of the college, and thirteen times when various rectors were absent for a considerable time, he was again in charge as vice-rector. But now for the moment he was free of the responsibilities of command, and could go seeking the strayed sheep in the alleys and the slave-pens, the hospitals and the jails, and in the long fatiguing hours in his besieged confessional.

THE record of Bernardine Realino's life up to the day of his leaving secular employment is shadowy and sparse compared to the sharp and detailed view we have of him as a Jesuit. In giving an account of his forty-two years in Lecce, the biographer must make his selection from a mass of evidence. There are Bernardine's abundant letters—to his superiors, to his brother Giambattista, to those who wrote asking for his advice. There are the records of the College of Lecce, preserved in the Jesuit archives in Lecce and Naples and Rome. And there are the testimonies gathered by the informational processes set on foot shortly after Father Realino's death, with a view to his beatification.

On this cross-hatching of document and incident and impression, the portrait of a man is imaged forth as clearly as if it had been painted by Bronzino or Holbein. It bears some striking resemblances to a young humanist who proudly wore the sword of a Duke's household, who had no paltry impression of his own talents and prospects, who had drawn blood in a sword-brawl, and nearly gone mad at the death of his sweetheart.

Some biographers have opined that Bernardine was so ashamed at the act of violence which had caused him to leave Carpi two jumps ahead of the bailiffs, that thereafter he smothered his emotions and became actually phlegmatic. It is true that he so schooled his feelings that his rare outbursts of anger were reserved for those who would make a principle of severity and turn cruelty into a civic virtue. And vanity and self-seeking had been burnt out of him by suffering and prayer. But the pure metal that remained was the original bronze and gold. He had lost none of his emotional ardor, but, where before it ran in rivulets of pride and ambition and human friendship, it was gathered now in one stream of love. He was a man who had traded all his substance for love, and love was all he had to give. He was not surprised when he found that love was what Lecce needed most.

Shortly after his arrival he had written to Father Salmeron:

I have been hardly three days in this city and already a great number have asked to go to confession. I have received them with open arms, led by an irresistible desire—and I do not think it is an illusion—to sacrifice myself for the salvation of these wonderful people.

Bernardine was an *operarius*, which is the name given to Jesuits who are assigned to one of the churches of the Society with the duties of saying Mass, preaching and catechizing, hearing confessions and administering the other sacraments, and visiting the sick and prisoners. He is the first Jesuit *operarius* to be canonized.

Though at his coming to Lecce he had been taken up by the wealthy and powerful, his first visits after paying his respects to the diocesan authorities, were to the city prisons. There were two of them—the Prison of the Governorship and that of the *Regia Udienza* or King's Bench. What the difference between them was is not clear, though it is a good conjecture that the former accommodated ordinary felons—thieves, murderers, debtors; and the King's Bench Prison housed tax evaders, smugglers and spies. It should be noted that, except for debtors, detention in these jails was not commonly the matter of the sentence; the prisoners were awaiting judgment which would either acquit them or send them to execution, mutilation, or to forced labor, usually in the galleys. The responsibility of the jailers was to deliver the prisoners safely to the courts, not, it appears, to feed them. For food and drink they had to look to the charity of friends or others.

Father Realino became the apostle of the prisons, bringing material as well as spiritual comfort into the hot, dank cells where the wretches awaited the pleasure of the courts. If a prisoner was utterly without friends, he did not hesitate to accompany him before the judge, and to plead for mercy.

A society called the Charity Confraternity brought the prisoners food twice a week. Bernardine often joined them at the house near one of the prisons where the food was prepared, and he carried wood and water and washed the pots and sliced the bread and gave such excellent opinions on the quality of the spaghetti and the use and abuse of garlic that the other amateur cooks made him head of the organization. He took on himself the responsibility of procuring water for one of the jails which had no dependable well. It was a matter of going around to the houses nearby and arranging that several families in turn would bring a big bucket of water to the prison each day. The custom continued for a long time, until the Jesuits had a cistern built in the prison.

Father Realino's greatest service to the prisoners was his devotion to the condemned. Before long it was he who went with every convict sentenced to death and remained with him until the state had exacted its barbarous toll. How much of a hardship the terrible experiences were to his sensitive spirit we may judge from one incident, the one that began his work as chaplain to the condemned.

A prisoner who had been sentenced to torture and death was being carried to execution through the streets of Lecce. Bernardine chanced on the scene in all its gruesome details: the prisoner chained down on a low wagon, the executioners tearing at his flesh with red-hot pincers. Bernardine recognized the condemned man as one who had refused to make his confession. With a cry of pity the Saint leaped into the cart. There was little time to lose; he must overwhelm this poor wretch with such a tide of paternal love that it would wash his sins away almost in spite of himself. Heedless of the glowing tongs, Bernardine threw his arms around the howling prisoner, whispering words of affection, and promises of mercy and eternal deliverance: beyond the mocking crowd and the waiting gallows, and the last minutes of suffering, see Christ Our Lord with His arms outstretched in welcome. Then as the prisoner hesitated, Bernardine kissed his smoking wounds and licked them like a hound. Before the strangler's rope cut short the agony a few minutes later, the man had whispered his confession and received absolution.

Slaves as well as prisoners pressed an old claim on his charity, but here in Lecce the status of the slaves was different. Since the city was not a port as Naples was, there would be hardly any galley slaves to be dealt with, but only Moors purchased for domestic service. There was more leisure to instruct them, and their condition was not so abject as that of the wretches who labored chained to an oar. In one of his early sermons in Lecce, Bernardine spoke plainly to those who regarded the Moorish bondsmen as an inferior species of man, a chattel to be used up in work in the fields or over the smoky kitchen fires. God recognized no distinction between the souls of master and slave, Father Realino reminded them. The good news of the gospel was for all, and he intended to seek out each Moor in the district and attempt to convert him.

He encountered little opposition on the part of the slave-owners, but there were thorny barriers to conversion in the disparity of language, and in hostility to Christianity, especially on the part of those slaves who were convinced Mahometans. Some of the dusky catechumens learned quickly and made steady progress, and among Bernardine's contemporaries the opinion was frequently held that the Saint had the gift of tongues—that he knew all the dialects spoken by the slaves and that they understood him even though he spoke in Italian. In general, this does not seem to have been the case, and we know that Bernardine sent for a Turkish grammar and at least once used an interpreter.

The work called out all his reserves of patience. Once it took him five days, working three hours a day, to teach a slave the words: "Hail, Mary, full of grace." His lay-brother companion finally said, "Oh, let him alone, Father, don't waste your time on him. Don't you see that this Negro is unable to learn anything?"

Bernardine replied, "He can't learn because the devil gets in the way. We must overcome the devil by patience."

A priest who had heard of the incident mentioned it that night to Realino. "It was very edifying to me, Father Bernardine, to hear that you broke your head today to teach four words of a prayer to a slave." On the contrary, Bernardine rejoined, it was the slave who deserved the credit, because he had shown no sign of impatience or fatigue during all the hours of instruction.

When a slave was sufficiently instructed and had freely asked for baptism, Bernardine arranged for a ceremony surrounded with all the solemnity he could muster. Usually it was held in the Cathedral and the new Christian was brought back to his home in a procession with music and banners and a guard of honor of prominent citizens.

Late in 1599 a Jew came over from Corfu to be received into the Church. Bernardine instructed him and saw him baptized on the first day of the new century. Then, since the convert spoke fluent Turkish, he was able to give some assistance in the instruction of the slaves.

How many slaves were converted? There is no available record of the total; Father Germier's estimate of two hundred seems highly reasonable and astounding enough if one considers the expenditure of fortitude and unwearied love required for each conquest. "He is a saint," the governor of the province of Lecce said when he came on Bernardine in the College garden, sitting surrounded by little Negro children. It was a judgment in which all Lecce was beginning to concur. And they did not forget that he had said that they must not spare him.

One night Bernardine was hurriedly called to assist a dying young woman. As he hurried through the gloomy streets he gathered some of the details from the two neighbors who had come for him after several other priests had refused the summons. It was a case of attempted murder over a matter of family honor —a crime not unusual in Lecce at that time. The barbarous custom was that if an unmarried woman became pregnant, one of her relatives must wipe out the blot on the family's good name by killing her.

Father Realino found the girl lying apparently near death from a score of stab-wounds inflicted by her brother. Bernardine heard her confession and assured her that she would not die, a prediction which her relatives received as a grim joke. But the young woman recovered and was able to leave the city. The incident was repeated many times, though Father Realino bitterly assailed the mad, savage pride that would not stop at murder. For a number of the unfortunate young women who appealed to him for help he was able to find some refuge where they would be safe from the vengeance of their families.

A young man came to him one day in great agitation and asked his advice: should he kill his sister, who was obviously approaching an unsanctioned childbirth, or should he let stern duty yield to natural affection? Bernardine listened quietly, his heart aching at the sabotage of character that prejudice and ignorance could work. He recognized the young man as one he had frequently seen in church. "A difficult case," Father Realino agreed, "a difficult case, my dear. Be good enough to wait and see what advice I shall give you." And he went into his room to pray, leaving the boy fidgeting in the corridor of the College. After four hours, Bernardine came out of his room smiling and with good news for the young man, who was almost ready to explode with impatience. His sister had given birth to a boy who had died quickly, after being baptized. Since the incident was now closed, there was no need to think about revenge. And he added that the young woman would be honorably married in about forty days.

When this astounding information was verified, the wonder grew, and the calls on Father Realino's charity were multiplied. Though he had repeatedly asked his superiors to send him to the foreign missions, he realized that as a stay-at-home Xavier his tasks were not unlike those confronting the Jesuits laboring in India or South America. For one instance, there was the rampant superstition that had him inveighing frequently against belief in charms and spells and the evil eye. He urged the devotion to the Holy Angels as an antidote to this pinchbeck diablerie.

Though he preached against the evils of the place and time, decrying the dishonesty of money-lenders and the excesses of the pleasure-mad, he was not content with the easy fireworks of moral indignation. He knew that the dry rot in the ark of the Church was ignorance, and he set out to teach his hearers the meaning of the Creed. Mere parading of metaphysics in the pulpit galled him like the stone. In the great variety of topics he expounded (one of his sermon courses was on the Our Father and another on the Mass) he would cite Democritus and Heraclitus, Aristotle and Aquinas, and yet he never lost sight of the common level of understanding: the man who could not read. The points he made were as clear and unmistakable as a highwayman's challenge. The sentences marched like trained infantry, and occasionally, when the trumpets of rhetoric were blowing, galloped like cavalry.

He was more at home in the direction and formation of individual souls; his mission was not to the multitudes but to a multitude of individuals. It was his great consolation to see the restoration of faith and fervor that the College was working in Lecce. The students, he wrote to Giambattista, "are taught not only literature but also Christian customs, how to pray, the use of the holy sacraments; so they go forth as trained soldiers to the war against the world, the flesh and the devil."

Bernardine sought for a means to give direction and continuity to the spiritual training imparted, to extend the spiritual influence of the College to the alumni and then to others in widening circles of age and social position. He felt the urgent need of trustworthy assistants with whom he could share the works of mercy he had begun in hospitals and prisons, among the slaves and the afflicted of every sort. The instrument he chose was the Sodality of Our Lady. It was an organization which had already proved its worth in the Jesuit college in Messina, where the first sodality had been founded in 1560, and at the Roman College, where the Belgian scholastic, Jean Leunis, established in 1563 the sodality that was to receive papal approbation in 1584 as the primary and central organization to which all other sodalities were to be affiliated. For Bernardine, the College was the natural point of departure. Sodalities were founded for the older and younger students, and later others were formed for various classes in the city—seven in all, including one for gentlemen (a counterpart of the famous Nobles' Sodality of Naples and Rome) and one for parish priests.

Still extant is the lengthy rule that Bernardine wrote for the gentlemen's sodality: "The Sodality of the Most Holy Annunciation of the Blessed Virgin Mary in the College of the Society of Jesus in the magnificent City of Lecce." Its main provisions applied also to the other sodalities. Each member was to seek his own spiritual perfection, and as far as possible that of his family, under the direction of the Jesuits; to engage in works of charity for the benefit of others, particularly for the poor of the city. A quarter-hour of meditation each day, recitation of the Little Office of the Blessed Virgin or the rosary, daily attendance at Mass or at least a visit to the Blessed Sacrament, and an examination of conscience each night were required. There was a general Communion on the first Sunday of each month, and the members were encouraged to communicate oftener. Special devotional practices were prescribed for Saturdays and Sundays, when the sodalities met, for Christmas and Lent and the time of Carnival.

Sick members were visited daily and public and private prayers were offered for their recovery. Committees were appointed to visit the sick in homes and hospitals, to instruct prisoners in the jails and exhort them to confession, to beg alms to liberate poor debtors, to settle law suits out of court, to collect clothing for distribution to the poor. Two sodalists went each week among the beggars and the street Arabs.

The city was astonished at the sight of the sons of merchants and nobles gathering the children for catechism, carrying food to the poor, leading the litany of Our Lady in the dank prisons or the stinking hospital wards. Bernardine understood the danger of smugness in all this, but he knew the value of any means for bridging the gap between corrosive poverty and the blithe opulence of the upper classes.

The sodality for priests was the heart of Bernardine's work for the reform of religious communities and the parish clergy in Lecce. There was a large population of nuns and friars in the city, but in many of them the essential spiritual motives for choosing the religious life were entirely lacking: unmarriageable daughters or unpromising younger sons, they had become religious under the pressure of their relatives.

It must not be thought that wanton evil stalked through the cloisters of Lecce, but in many cases the primitive observance of the religious rule had been given up in important particulars. Interminable visits from friends and relatives, private gifts, servants, endless calculations of personal advantage—these had made some of the convents little Balkan kingdoms of jealousy and bickering. It was Bernardine's task to restore the wayward communities to the necessary context of prayer and recollection and penance, to insist upon silence and the observance of cloister, and to war against idleness, the slow poison of the religious spirit. First in two convents where the Vicar Capitular had sent him in his first year in Lecce, and then in other religious houses, he carried on his work of restoration by conference and exhortation and the grace of the sacrament of penance. His training as a canonist and confessor and all his apostolic kindness and wisdom were required to deal with the conditions he found. To rescue religious who were in difficult straits or to separate from religious life those who were irrevocably committed to making the best of two worlds, he did not hesitate to ask faculties and dispensations from the highest authority in Rome.

The sodality for priests was Bernardine's sling and pebbles against the mailed and roaring Goliath of clerical incompetence. The Council of Trent had carefully explored the problem of the education of priests, and in a momentous decree had obliged the bishops to found a seminary in every diocese, or at least in each metropolitan see. Led by the luminous example of the German College, which St. Ignatius had founded in Rome in 1552, the seminaries were sending out priests trained in scripture and theology, schooled to a high ideal of zeal and personal sanctity. They were desperately needed. The practice of dragooning youngsters into the clergy to keep a rich benefice in the family; the ordination of children to the priesthood or even making them bishops, the custom of taking Orders after a haphazard apprenticeship in the house of a parish priest—these had raised red havoc with the awesome responsibilities of the priesthood.

The College at Lecce, with its classes in philosophy and theology open to laymen as well as clerics, was not intended to be a seminary, though it did produce a number of excellent candidates for the priesthood. Bernardine was anxious to be of some service to those already ordained; the success of his sodalities for laymen impelled him to inaugurate one for priests as a means of fostering the priestly virtues and to provide some instruction as well. The rule he wrote reveals the high degree of earnestness and self-consecration required of the members, and suggests that Father Realino was not impressed by mere numbers.

The priest sodalists undertook to meditate for a half hour each day, to celebrate Mass and recite the Divine Office with devotion and according to the Roman manner, to examine their conscience each night, to confess at least each week. Obedience to the hierarchy was inculcated and concern for the good estate of the Church was made practical in the prayers prescribed for Pope and bishops, for Christian rulers, for the conversion of the Sultan of Turkey and the Queen of England. This internal renovation was to issue in a more intense devotion to the spiritual assistance of the faithful.

The priests' sodality, which Bernardine hoped would spread to every Jesuit college, probably had no more than fifty members in the Saint's lifetime. It endured for two hundred years, in varying states of fervor, until the Jesuits were swept out of the Kingdom of Naples by the Bourbons. It remains only as a memory and a landmark in the Italian Counter-Reformation: the first sodality for priests founded under Jesuit auspices.

To assist the priests in the all-important ministry of the confessional, Bernardine inaugurated clerical conferences for instruction in moral theology and the solution of typical confessional problems. This was close on the year 1583, which saw the founding of the priests' sodality; the sodality meeetings and the moral theology conferences seem to have been held in alternate weeks, with the latter open to all priests whether sodalists or not. The Jesuit archives in Rome possess a copy of the instructions given by Bernardine at the conferences. The 323 closely written pages are eloquent witness to the depth of his knowledge of moral theology and canon law, and his wide familiarity with the authorities in those fields, as well as to the resolute judgment and the ardent quality of mercy which made him the incomparable confessor.

The growing demands upon him, particularly in the confessional, made Bernardine grateful for reliable auxiliaries who multiplied his hands and poured the oil and wine into the city's wounds in Christ's name, and however much he would protest, in his name too. Some works of mercy he would not delegate and unaccountably, he found time for them in his crowded days. Each week he would go over to the poorest section of the city, to a teeming Hogarthian street where a paralyzed boy lived with his mother in a rickety house that was more like a shed, with a thatched roof and an earthen floor. "Come," Father Realino would say to the brother who accompanied him, "let us make our visit to my dear little boy."

The child would hear them coming and would call out in his piping voice, "Here comes the holy man! How's the holy man?" The gentle Saint would sit by the bedside with the liquid black eyes of the child upon him as he opened the basket of gifts he had brought: oranges that some magnifico had sent Father Realino from his orchard; almonds covered with sugar and dyed the color of robins' eggs, and a live hare that made the child cry out with delight.

"This boy is the saint, Bernardine is the sinner," Realino would whisper to the brother as they turned to leave.

If we have observed that he does not seem to have been at home in the pulpit, his heart was surely in the teaching of catechism.[1] Though he was a doctor of both laws he was proud to be chosen to break the news of redemption to little children; to be able to tell them that God loved Lecce and every runny-nosed Leccean child. What a privilege to have seen him go by on a fresh spring morning on his way to catechism class, nodding and smiling as the men lifted their hats and the women bowed and crossed themselves and solemnly kissed their thumbs, and the children skipped along beside him or begged a *santina*—a brightly colored holy card.

The hair that was once the color of autumn honey is now white, and his full face is framed by a white beard, closely clipped. His nose is short for a Lombard's, with a little of the eagle in it. The broad, lean frame in the shabby cassock is stooped, so that even at fifty he sometimes leans on a long staff.

He goes down the Via dei Tribunali and the Via Augusto Imperatore with cross-streets giving glimpses of the sumptuous baroque mansions standing among the olive and palm trees, and then the alleys of the poor where the families and the family's donkey are huddled in a few wretched rooms. The Piazza Sant' Oronzo is a great vat of sunlight as he crosses it, the colors of the morning as bright as wet tile: the golden stone of the buildings, the gray and white and blue of the wheeling pigeons, the brightly dyed wares of the cloth market spread on rows of low tables in the middle of the square, where St. Oronzo stands at the top of his tall column, giving a bronze blessing. The Via Ascanio Grande leads west, past the convent of the Poor Clares with its steep flight of

[1] In the decree of beatification, Leo XIII compared Bernardine to St. Philip Neri in his love for children: "Both loved their neighbor with glowing charity, especially children with whom these holy men became children again, and whom they did not cease to train up in the precepts of the Gospel until an advanced old age."

steps and elaborately carved entrance flanked by Corinthian columns. In the Piazza del Duomo, the Bishop's palace stands beside the Cathedral, the high entrance door crowned with the arms of Aragon and the heraldic wolf of Lecce.

The beadle rings the bronze bell as Bernardine enters the great hall and the surging, screaming maelstrom of children subsides into a pool of angelic faces, with only a few eddies of fighting on the outer edges. Father Realino makes a man-sized sign of the Cross and the lesson begins. The Our Father and the Hail Mary and the Creed are chanted again and again; for a respite one of the better pupils engages in a dialogue with a little inquirer called the *ignoto*. Then Father Realino gives a short sermon and leads the drill on the catechism questions.

"Are you a Christian?" he asks. It is the first question in the little catechism he uses. And the answer comes back, soprano and tenor and uncertain fourteen-year-old bass, in a thundering chorus to make beleaguered Christendom take heart: "Yes, by the grace of Our Lord Jesus Christ, I am!"

Robert Francis Romulus Bellarmine was so marvelously many-sided that it is not strange that his Protestant adversaries spread the report that he was not one person but several writing under one name. As lecturer and Rector of the Roman College and author of the polemical *De Controversiis,* more than any other single man he wove the sinews of war for the intellectual rally of the Counter-Reformation. It was a dubious reward when he was taken from the Roman College at the end of 1594 and sent to Naples as Provincial for a three-year term.

Bellarmine, besides being the peerless knight of the Holy See, a Doctor of the Church and a great democrat into the sublime bargain, was as gentle and lovable a little man as you could meet in a day's journey. Deep was calling to deep, then, in the early months of his administration, when he nominated Father Realino as the Rector of the College of Lecce. Father General Claudio Acquaviva assented, and with the hasty protocol by which Jesuit superiors are inducted, the decree of installation was read at dinner in the College refectory, and Bernardine got up from his place and took the Rector's chair.

A few days later he gave an exhortation, the first of several addresses he would be required to make to the Jesuit community each year. It expresses so clearly his view of the responsibility of a religious superior that we shall quote it at some length. He began:

Love needs no exordium. And surely if exordium serves only to assure the benevolence of the hearers, I do not see any need of it with my own fathers and brothers, who love me, as I know, with their whole heart, such is their goodness and virtue. . . . Forgetting the fine words then, I shall say that since God Our Lord, and His vicar in our Society, who is our more than lovable Father General, has placed me in charge of the vineyard—that is, has wished to give me, when I least expected it, the care of this College, in which each one of the subjects is a vine-shoot planted and carefully nurtured by the divine hand, I freely accept with all my too evident unworthiness: "The chalice which the Father has given me, shall I not drink it?"

The governance of the Society is all love, all charity . . . and to attain this purpose the Society has various excellent means, but I shall touch briefly on only three of them. The first is this in the rules of the Father Rector . . . that it be his primary care to support the whole college, all without exception, priests or brothers, high or low, all with prayer and holy desires.

The second important point is that very often he speak with his subjects with a great manifestation of love (hence it is not enough to have it hidden in his heart). . . .

The third point is that he take care that the constitutions and rules be observed. . . . This is the principal requirement for a successful administration. There is only one thing I would observe under this head, that the great gentleness of the Society can be seen even in this particular, since with all its solicitude for the observance of the rules, it allows the superior when it is necessary—when a real need occurs (which is understood, as I said, with moral prudence), to grant a dispensation from all the constitutions, from all the rules, from all the ordinances. What kindness that is! "Who is weak and I am not weak?" So it is clear that our rule is paternal.

One biographer of Realino adds that in this opening exhortation the Saint said: "Do not consider me your superior but rather as the servant of all of you."

From the beginning of the two-year term as Rector, and during various intervals when he governed the College as Vice-rector, Bernardine made it clear that he literally believed that as superior he should be the servant of the whole house. In waiting on table and reading to the community during meals he took his turn with the other Jesuits, and often substituted for the inevitable missing waiter. It was not uncommon to find him in the scullery, washing plates and pans, or answering the jangling doorbell in place of the porter. In the sacristy he would help priests to vest, and then serve their Masses. Before a sermon or a lecture he would be in the Church arranging the chairs. When the brother *excitator* was sick one winter, he filled in for some time, going from door to door in the chilly corridors before dawn, knocking and saying "*Benedicamus Domino!*" and listening for the sleepy "*Deo gratias*" from within. He often helped out on wash day, carrying in water from the well, and wood for the laundry stove, and then lugging out the baskets of wet washing and hanging it on the clothesline.

Even when he was eighty, and Vice-rector again, he came to the kitchen to help the brother cook wash the dishes. The minister of the house and one of the consultors came down to remonstrate with him—carrying in pails of water was clearly beyond his strength. Bernardine demurred and said that he would like to continue his work. The minister declared that he could command him to stop exerting himself beyond his strength. This was too much.

"And I am Vice-rector," responded Bernardine, smiling, "and if you don't get out of here I'll give you a penance."

Of course he was imposed on, but for all that he lost none of his generosity and his simple trust in the goodness of his subjects. When a lay brother asked him to copy out a rather long section from a spiritual book, Bernardine readily agreed and began to write the passage in a notebook. A scholastic inquired whether Father Realino was at work on some composition of his own, and when the truth came out, exclaimed, "The brother needs a good penance to knock some sense into his head. Here, give the book to me; I'm younger than you."

"No, no," Bernardine replied. "This good brother has asked me to do something for his spiritual profit."

He was no less gentle and tactful in correcting infractions of the rules. It was unheard-of for him to speak a harsh word. If he came upon someone breaking a rule, he would merely look lovingly at him and pass on. He delayed fifteen days before admonishing a lay brother who had excoriated a priest for keeping the people waiting for Mass. Once when a lay brother had been guilty of some offense that had given bad example, Bernardine commanded him to take the discipline in the refectory in the presence of the community. It was a rather severe but not an uncommon penance. The brother went through the house complaining bitterly against Father Realino, whose only reaction was to send him word that he would not have to perform the penance after all. But that night at supper when grace was said and the community sat down with a scraping of chairs and flourishing of napkins, Bernardine stood at the superior's place and asked the brother's pardon for having caused him any suffering. It was a scene of such saintly humility and selfless courtesy that many wept, and the lay brother was completely won over.

Though he realized that it was his duty to enforce the rules, yet he never forgot that as superior he could waive any one of them. During one hot summer he noticed that when the bell rang for the end of evening recreation, some of the Jesuits still remained chatting in the garden, reluctant to go indoors. And the rule which forbade eating and drinking between meals without permission was being infringed by some who were drinking water because of the heat. Bernardine suspended the rule to allow the water-drinking and lengthened the evening recreation. Similarly, when he saw that the rule forbidding the hearing of confessions while a sermon was in progress, was a hardship to priests and penitents, he appealed to the Provincial and the General with the result that the regulation was suspended for greater feast days and finally, at Bernardine's urging, dispensed with entirely for the Lecce Gesù.

It was the sick who realized most clearly what it was to have a saint for a superior. He came to the infirmary ten or a dozen times a day, and if the patient was depressed, would exert all his energies to make him smile at a joke. Even when he was an old man he brought up the food to the infirmary, made beds and swept rooms and performed all manner of humble offices for the bedridden. He would rise two or three times in the night to see whether bandages were secure or the patient restless. If the sickness was severe he would watch all night at the bedside and in the morning go cheerfully about his other work.

Every exertion in the classroom or in the ministry was rewarded with his genuine interest and praise: the priest who had delivered a well-prepared sermon, the scholastic who had defended his thesis against all comers in a disputation, the brother who had cooked the Sunday goose to perfection. He was at pains that his subjects would be well-clothed, and would give away his own biretta or his cassock without a moment's thought. An ancient patched cassock was good enough for him, because, he explained quite transparently, the fresh dye in new clothes would smudge off on his hands.

Visitors were given a smiling welcome and brought ceremoni-

ously to their rooms, often enough with Father Realino carrying
the baggage. If the guests were especially travel-weary, or had
come on foot, Bernardine would bring up a basin of water and
give them the ancient courtesy of washing their feet.

It was not surprising that the College became known as an ideal
Jesuit community, and that Father Provincial in Naples was pes-
tered by requests for transfer to Lecce. Bellarmine came down to
Lecce himself during Bernardine's first year as Rector. Father
Brodrick describes the arrival of St. Robert, and compares it to
the meeting of St. Francis and St. Dominic. All the Jesuits had
come down to the door to welcome him with the customary kiss
of peace. Bellarmine jumped off his horse and before anyone could
open his mouth, demanded, "Which of you is Father Bernardine?"

Bernardine was trying unsuccessfully to go unnoticed in the
midst of the group, but now he was pushed forward. The humble
rector went on his knees and lifted his head to find that Father
Bellarmine had knelt also, moved by identical motives of reverence and love.

That day began a friendship which was to last until Bernardine's
death, though he was to see Father Bellarmine only once more in
the flesh, when the Provincial made his second visitation to Lecce
in the following year. Bellarmine made a general confession of
his whole life to Father Realino, and often thereafter wrote for
his advice and spiritual direction, especially when he was raised
to the cardinalate and made Archbishop of Capua. As his works
came from the press he would send them to Lecce, begging Bernardine's prayers to help him in the battle of the books.

Long afterward, when Bernardine had gone to heaven a few
years before him, Cardinal Bellarmine declared that if he had been
Pope he would have proclaimed Bernardine blessed immediately
after his death. And the valiant Cardinal, who could number his
own antagonists in battalions, made moving testimony to the uni-
versal affection for his friend. "Others of the saints," he said, "have
been at times an object of aversion and dislike, and occasions were
always found for some complaint and murmuring against them,
which God permits to put their patience and humility to the test.
But I have never heard a single complaint about Father Realino,
though I have been his Provincial; even those who were ill-disposed

to the Society, who seized every opportunity to speak unfavorably of it . . . always made exception for Realino. No one, they said, can say anything but good about him. Everyone knows that he is a saint." [1]

It was a sanctity laid in the dimension that Blessed John Ruysbroeck described by saying, "Be kind, be kind, and you will be saints." Bernardine never forgot that Christ made the corporal works of mercy a matter of devotion to His own Person: "I was naked and you covered me; I was a stranger and you took me in." Taking Christ wholeheartedly at His word, he found it impossible to resist any appeal for assistance, no matter how high the tax it laid on his own comfort. "I feel that love is multiplied in the same measure as responsibility is enlarged," he said in an exhortation to the community. As Rector he was now at liberty to place the resources of the College at the service of the poor. The porter and the procurator were instructed never to send a needy person away without a donation. Bread and soup and a cup of the good wine of Lecce were given to all who asked, and whatever other food was available. If the oranges were ripe in the College garden, Bernardine would gather them himself for his dear poor. If no other means sufficed, he would go through the city begging for clothing and food. He was especially generous with those who had once been people of means and to whom begging was a violent embarrassment. When he was not superior Bernardine would save the greater part of his own dinner for some poor person. And he would gather what food was left at the table and distribute it at the College door.

More than once sick men who were penniless were brought into the College. Once a man from Bari, who was lodging in a cheap hotel in Lecce, became seriously ill. Alone and desperate, with all his money gone, he sent a message to Father Realino asking for help. Bernardine, who was then Superior, wished to bring him into the College and asked his consultors for their opinion. They were all opposed: some of the Jesuits were sick, there was

[1] The Jesuits at Lecce used to recall a truculent anti-clerical who was a fierce despiser of the Society. Whenever in his conversation he would damn the Jesuits to hell-fire, he would carefully specify that his anathemas did not apply to Father Bernardine.

no room for a stranger, and no one to care for him. Bernardine said that there was always room for charity, that the man could take his own room if necessary, and he himself was ready to care for him. So Father Realino had the sick man brought to the College on a stretcher, found him a room, and cared for him for twenty-two days, until the man was ready to take the road again.

On another occasion a Frenchman fell into the same straits in Lecce, and though Realino was not governing the College, he prevailed on the Rector to take the stranger in. He was there about six weeks, and at his departure Bernardine provided him with a suit of clothes and a horse for the long journey back to France.

Some of the fathers of the College once remonstrated with Father Realino and assured him that his extravagant charities would see the community in want. The College charged its students nothing and depended on donations and its slender endowment. With Father Realino as Rector, gifts seemed to flow through the house like the Tiber in flood. Bernardine listened gravely to the complaint and then responded mildly enough: "Oh, men of little faith; to give to the poor is to lend to the Lord, and when we give to Him, He rewards a hundredfold."

Bernardine's critics could not deny that this holy spendthrift, who scattered his largesse on all the winds of heaven, had built in an incredibly short time a magnificent church and a spacious college. To be sure, there was a debt, that familiar gray wolf that sleeps on the doorstep of most Catholic colleges; but Bernardine had no fear for the future. "Always give and fear nothing," he said. "God will provide for the needs of His servants."

A Monsignor Torrisio, Bishop of Segna, suggested to him that he could easily pay off the College's debts by writing to devout people, especially in Naples, and requesting donations. The letters would be prized as relics, the Bishop added frankly. Bernardine replied quickly that God did not require this of him and it was not his habit to bother people with requests of this kind.

The truth was that Father Realino did not believe that the College was to be supported by ducats from duchesses, but by the prayer and penance and the consecrated labor of the members of the community. In an exhortation to his fellow Jesuits he said:

I want to say that it is through love that devotion in prayer is kept strong. If there is no fire in the kitchen, there is a rather bleak prospect in the refectory. If the natural heat of the body diminishes, what hope is there of preserving life? Prayer is the tree of life which conserves and restores the life of the soul. It is by this, as our Holy Father Ignatius tells us, that our College is supported. We deceive ourselves if we think that our income supports the College. If the house were in danger of falling and we had to hold it up with our hands, certainly every father and brother would rush to give his assistance. Do we not see that if a father or brother is sick, everyone runs to wait on him? . . . And will we not do likewise for the spiritual conservation, the spiritual sustenance of the College?

Bernardine's charity was not restricted to human beings: he had a childlike affection for birds. The sight of a caged bird distressed him, and he did what he could to have the poor prisoned things released. In the winter he would spread crumbs on his window-sill, and in the warmer months, when the casements were open, the birds would come in and perch on his shoulders or his hands—fat duennas of pigeons with coral feet and iridescent collars, pert soubrettes of wrens and swallows, and sparrows as saucy as street Arabs.

"Don't these winged guests bother you?" someone asked.

"Not at all," Bernardine protested. "They are a source of admiration and comfort to me. They remind me of the goodness of the heavenly Father Who nourishes all His creatures."

It was proverbial that he spoke ill of no one but the devil. He was reluctant to believe evil about anyone, and if he could not deny it he would say, "I am a worse ingrate toward God, and if His invisible hand had not restrained me, I would commit greater crimes." When a prince, the governor of the province, criticized the conduct of a bishop, Bernardine told him bluntly: "I do not think it is possible in such a man, but let us suppose that it were true: who can ever be sure of a man's intentions? But you who are set over others and apart from others ought to be better than they; you ought not to believe, much less to say such things."

From the day of his grand-opera entrance until his death forty-two years later, Bernardine did not leave Lecce. For all that, his interests never became parochial. The horizons of his fraternal love were set far beyond the spires and the chimney pots of the city. Some saints who were cast in a less lovable mold made the complete separation from family part of their stern asceticism. Bernardine saw no contradiction between love of friends and family and the love of God. He kept in contact with his home city, and his letters to his brother in Carpi are the best source of information about his daily life. He never lost his boyish delight at receiving letters from home, and he shared Chesterton's wonder at the "miracle of the mailbox." In one letter to his brother he wrote: "Blessed be Our Lord, Who by the gift of writing makes present those who are far away and lets those communicate with each other whom mountains and seas divide. Your letters always bring me great consolation." Once he reminded his brother to pray for the safety of the post-riders who brought the mailbags tedious distances, through danger and storm.

He was intensely interested in his nephews and concerned that they be competently educated. A letter from Carpi announcing the birth of another nephew drew this jubilant reply:

When the regular mail arrived from Naples, as it does every eighth day, there were several letters for me and among them yours of the first of December with another of my dear Francesco.[2] I immediately recognize the handwriting in the address, and joy wells in my heart. . . . I open it and read, and behold, here is the good news of a boy-child, a new Ignatius! The lady mother of the child is safe, and the boy, as if risen from the dead, is baptized at home; then at the church the good Don Geminiano supplies the rest of the sacred rites. I assure you that I at once went on my knees at the oratory which we all have in our rooms and I said the sacred litanies of our Blessed Lady, and thanked God for this singular favor.

The letters went out in their incredible volume to Jesuits too, and reveal Bernardine's intense interest in every work of the Society. He found time to write to his brethren on the foreign missions, the letters full of affectionate references to Jesuits in the home provinces and innocent ecclesiastical gossip. The reports of

[2] Father Tiraboschi's *Biblioteca Modenese* records the fact that this nephew Francesco came twice to Lecce to see his famous uncle, and was present at Father Realino's death.

the missionaries, published in Rome, he would have read in the refectory; if there were some notable achievements recorded—a pagan tribe converted or a native "king" baptized—he would declare a holiday for the community.

A letter to Giambattista announces the arrival of the Jesuits in China in 1583:

We have received word that our fathers have entered China with the permission of the King, and are preaching our holy faith and baptizing, where before the name of Christ the Redeemer was never heard, and idols were adored instead. It is a country of vast extent, 24,000 miles from Italy, much further than India, governed by a single King and speaking only one language. There is hope that this King will turn Christian, if it be Our Lord's will. This land is a new world in itself.

Another letter to his brother describes the arrival in Rome in 1585 of an embassy from Japan: two young Japanese princes, and two other knights, converts to the faith, come to do homage to the Holy Father. They had been received with great honor by the King of Spain and the Grand Duke of Florence, and were lodged with the Jesuits in the professed house at the Gesù in Rome. The gossipy old city was delighted with these strange, reserved youngsters, who were as fully Christian as if they had been reared in Italy. They were hailed to the Vatican with the honors reserved for princes, and the protocol of the apostolic court can be awe-striking indeed, for the Eternal City has never quite forgotten what a Roman triumph was.

The coming of the princes was a glorious reward for Gregory XIII's generosity and zeal for the missions, and there were tears in the old Pope's eyes as the Japanese lads knelt before him and he gently raised them and allowed them to kiss his hands. That was only a few weeks before Gregory's death. His successor, Sixtus V, did them further honor. Bernardine did not fail to report the rumor that His Holiness might make one of them a cardinal. A later letter was still buzzing with the same news, for the visit of the Japanese was one of the wonders of the century. They had been bidden to Mass in the Pope's chapel, and His Holiness communicated them with his own hand. They were made

Knights of St. Peter also, though the rumored red hat was not conferred.

In this memorable year of 1585, a young Jesuit scholastic was sent to the College of Lecce to teach mathematics. The eldest son of the Count of Tassarola, he had entered the novitiate at Nola the previous year with a vague ambition for service on the missions smouldering in his black-thatched head. The novitiate gave him pause; the missions were not all glamorous sight-seeing and heroic postures. He wondered whether his patrician breeding and bon-bon flesh were equal to the peril and the labor. He took his problem to Father Realino. Bernardine gave him no solution but only urged him to pray for divine light and to make good use of each day's graces. Then he watched while the novice prayed and taught long division and algebra and went into the streets to gather the children for catechism and, like a child amid the lions, preached earnest little sermons in the city prisons. The greater part of a year had gone by before Bernardine assured him that he should volunteer for foreign service.

"My son," Bernardine said, "write to Father General and tell him the longings of your heart. I'll support your petition in every way I can, for there is no doubt that God has destined you for Japan, and that you are called to do great things for Him there."

Years later, when Bernardine was dead and the Italian Jesuits were gathering the evidences of his sanctity, the India fleet brought a letter which was soon to be a relic in its own right. It was a moving testimony to Bernardine's holiness, signed by the Jesuit for whom he had predicted great things in Japan: Blessed Charles Spinola, martyred at Nagasaki in 1622.

FATHER REALINO at seventy might have retired in all conscience to some quiet novitiate to end his days in resolute leisure. His fame would be secure as the magistrate turned Jesuit, the servant of the poor, the chaplain of the forgotten and the damned in prisons and slave-pens, who had built a lordly college and a church in which the beauty of God's face cried in all the gates of the senses. If he had any such idea (and once, for a brief hour he dallied with the thought of a journey back to Carpi) Lecce was determined never to let him go. And Bernardine, to whom family affection was always a real and honorable thing, could not deny that he had made the whole city his kinsmen in the blood of Christ.

The attempts to remove him, at least for a time, to other Jesuit houses, had never quite ceased until his middle sixties. The circumstances which thwarted the commands of his superiors,—the fevers which confined him to his bed, or the violent storms that drove him back into the city on the two occasions when sickness did not intervene—these were proof enough to the Lecceans that God intended him to remain with them. Even so, they were taking no chances. The city council, that faithful weather vane in the winds of popular feeling, passed a decree prohibiting any assistance in Father Realino's attempted departure. Brother Giuseppe Soria testified to the further measures that were contemplated:

I remember still, for I witnessed it, that because of the great devotion which the whole city bore for Father Bernardine, every time that orders came from Rome or Naples that the said Father Bernardine should leave, the whole city was aroused, and was set against the said Father Bernardine's going. And I remember that once when he wished to go the mayor was Signor Cesare Bello, and another time the mayor was Signor Leonardo de Prato, and seeing that Father Bernardine was preparing to set out, they declared that they were ready to bar the gates of the city so that it would be impossible for him to leave.

From his fiftieth year, old age had set its mark upon him. The bent back and the pale, wrinkled face made him look older than he was. A kidney ailment gave him the back-ache occasionally, and he had a perpetual cold in the head which caused him to wear a cloth cap like an oversize skull-cap, except when he was saying Mass. Father General Acquaviva believed that the humid climate was unhealthy for him, and at the end of Bernardine's two-year term as rector, he made a final attempt to remove him from Lecce. Bernardine prepared to go, but again the fever struck him and Acquaviva, like his predecessors, had to yield to the inevitable. There is a hint that he intended to make Father Realino a provincial.

A lingering ear infection caused Bernardine some concern because deafness would limit his usefulness in the work which had claimed most of his efforts. As his physical powers decreased, his energies were gathered more and more in this one point: the hearing of confessions and the personal direction of souls.

In a letter to one of his nephews he wrote:

I devote much time to hearing confessions to purify souls from the slime of sin; it is a function quite angelic and quite beyond my powers, but since my superiors have imposed it on me I must obey, for having made a vow of obedience I must forget myself and trust only in my Savior.

How much pain this dedication cost him we can only surmise. He admitted to Father Muzio Vitelleschi, then Provincial of Naples, his profound repugnance for hearing confessions. Bernardine's reaction to this aversion was typically Ignatian. He would go against his own desires, making issue with self-love on the very ground where it was strongest. In every saint's life the crucifixion of Christ is in some way re-enacted. The confessional would be his Calvary, to be suffered daily without complaint or respite. He would be at the service of everyone, like a milestone or a bridge or a public well. His own feelings would not be considered—under peril of failure he could not allow them to be considered. Any signs of impatience or disgust in the exercise of his office of confessor would mar his effectiveness as a minister of Christ's mercy. He must put aside his own will and all calculations of personal advantage and be utterly at the service of sinners; he must be gentle with the coarse and the unclean; patient with those who were striking a queasy balance between fear and concupiscence; he must suffer fools gladly. "Obedience," he wrote, "gives us the desire and the ability for things which, without it, we could neither will nor attempt."

At dawn when the brother sacristan came to open the doors of the Gesù, Father Realino would already be kneeling in prayer before the altar. As the faithful gathered for Mass, he would seat himself in his confessional and the divine traffic of forgiveness began. He would begin in the half-dark of early morning, and the sun would be high in the heavens when the last of the morning's penitents had finished. In the summer he would say Mass at the latest and hottest hour, to save his brother priests this hardship, and in the winter the earliest Mass for the same reason. Sometimes the confessions went on for six or seven hours and individual penitents would ask to be heard at any hour of the day. On great feast days he spent eight or ten hours in the confessional.

Once he cried out under the burden. He had been called to the confessional many times in the day, and finally when the sacristan came tapping at his door again, Bernardine exclaimed impatiently that he was also under obligation to read his breviary. But the storm passed in a moment and he went serenely down to the church. Later he apologized to the brother for his conduct.

When Bernardine was hearing confessions all his attention was concentrated on his work, so that he did not attend to what was going on in the church. One Christmas Eve, when a large crowd had come for solemn Mass, a madman rushed bellowing into the Gesù, naked and waving a sword. The people fell back in terror, and surged screaming toward the doors. The man was soon overpowered and taken out of the church—and all the while Father Realino sat in his confessional, quite unaware of the riot in progress.

His clients were not limited to the Lecceans; gradually his reputation as a confessor spread and the files of penitents became longer. Many of them came from distant places, some of them prominent men who may have been discomforted to find that Father Bernardine enforced strict democracy in the waiting lines.

Once when a Marquis arrived with some pomp and circumstance he had to cool his heels while some ragged tramp was confessing to Bernardine. At another time the *avvocato fiscale* of the Province of Lecce took his place in the cue after a slave.

Inside the confessional also, Bernardine was the same to all. Everyone was received with the same Christlike gentleness and patiently listened to, and absolved with a few words of advice which gave a new vision of the incredible mercy of God. "In hating sin," he once wrote, "I do not hate the sinner—that would be to hate myself. God has deigned to give me compassion toward sinners; the greater sinners they are, the more ready am I to welcome them and listen to them in confession."

When he was asked one day whether a confessor should refuse absolution to one who falls repeatedly into the same serious sin, Bernardine replied: "The confessor can refuse, but he is not obliged to do it. The confession of the most hidden and serious sins is made at great cost to the penitent, and causes him considerable shame. When a sinner does violence to himself on this point and shows himself to the priest in this humiliating state, we can justly assume that he has been touched by grace and has been guided to confession by his guardian angel. Consequently, instead of treating him harshly, and putting off absolution, the confessor ought to try with all possible charity to arouse true contrition and a resolute purpose of amendment."

He liked to compare the confessor to a physician, whose purpose is the restoration of the sinner to health. Even when deep-seated habits of sin require strong remedies, the confessor should act with the care and delicacy of a surgeon operating on his own child.

One of Bernardine's contemporaries, a Father Francesco Mirabelli, said of him:

Never did he send anyone away from confession uncomforted, whether Jesuits or others, and this because of the charity which he showed in a special way for sinners. Though he was most austere with himself, he was all charity and sweetness towards them, especially when he saw that they were disposed to amend. I recall in this connection that he was displeased at certain severe opinions I held about confession, and he believed that confession should be made easy and not hedged about and made a burden. One time in a conference on typical cases of conscience, at which I presided, with the fathers from the College in attendance, I defended a rather strict opinion regarding formal contrition. Father Bernardine, with anger that seemed to spring entirely from charity and the desire to see everyone saved, publicly opposed my contention. When I cited many learned authors in support of my view, he said flatly that he did not care to hold any such opinion and that the road must be made easy for sinners when they begin to turn to repentance.

Besides his superb competence in moral theology and canon law, and his unswerving gentleness, Bernardine's success as a confessor was due to his phenomenal insight into souls. Some, before beginning their confession, were reminded of sins they had forgotten or were intending to conceal. Others were reproved because they had come to confession without the resolution of amendment. One man who had committed a terrible crime within his own family, and was tempted to murder to prevent public disclosure of his guilt, was overwhelmed with Father Realino's solicitude. "It was not you, my son, who committed this monstrous sin," Bernardine assured him, "but your corrupt nature. These are the results of our weakness." And the man was led to complete repentance, Bernardine promising him that the sin he had committed would not reach public notice.

Many times a dispute would be brought to Realino for judgment instead of to the civil court. Often he was called on to act as peacemaker. A man who had come to Lecce on business was quite inflamed with a desire for revenge, and would not have stopped at murder. One of the fathers of the College brought him to Bernardine's room, and the man gave an account of his grievance. The Saint asked him to kneel, and then placed his hands on his head and whispered, "Forgive, my brother, forgive freely, with all your heart, for the love of God. Say the *Pater* and *Ave* twice and I promise to recite the beads for you. And be at peace, because you will lose none of your honor." The man promised with tears to give up his grudge; not long afterwards his adversary came to ask his pardon.

One day while Mass was going on in the Gesù the square outside was filled with the clamor of a street brawl: the adherents of

the Mettola and Pratola families were clashing their swords and
screaming at each other like fishwives. This was only one of the
many raucous disputes which divided some of the prominent families of the city. It is a question just how much blood was spilt in
these Capulet and Montague encounters, but at least Christian
charity was wounded. Bernardine quietly undertook to settle the
quarrels and eventually prevailed with his prayers and his calm
reasoning and the inevitable assurance that both sides would lose
none of their honor. The Lubelli and the De Raino families agreed
to bury the hatchet, and Bernardine brought them together before the altar of the Gesù, where they exchanged the kiss of peace.
The widowed mother and the older brother of a young Leccean
who had been murdered kept the desire of revenge smouldering
for years afterwards. When the widow was about to get married
a second time, the bridegroom attempted to persuade her to put
the hatred out of her heart. He was unsuccessful until the woman
talked the matter out with Father Realino; she forgave the assas-
sins and promised to pray often for them.

Father Bernardine was successful in erasing all the longstand-
ing feuds between the prominent families in Lecce—a large achievement indeed, if we consider how hot the tempers ran in those
disputes, the deep roots of the antagonisms, and the feverish concern for family prestige. Even more important was his success in
reconciling hardened sinners with God. It was commonly held
that to have Father Realino at the bedside of the dying was a sure
guarantee of a holy death. Though the lines of penitents in the
church grew longer, he was still called at any hour to go to the
assistance of the dying.

A man who was a truculent enemy of religion had stoutly resisted attempts to convert him. When he was near death, his wom-
enfolk sent for Father Realino. It was early in the morning when
the Saint came into the man's room and was greeted by an angry
bellow from the patient, a great bulk of a man who lay panting
in the bed like a whale aground.

"What are you doing here? Who sent for you? Didn't I forbid
you ever to set foot in my house?"

"My friend," Bernardine said mildly, "both charity and duty
obliged me to visit my sick brother."

"I your friend, your brother?" The great body heaved over
in the bed, turning its back on the Saint.

"Yes, you are my brother. Each day I pray for you, that you
will return to your true self and that one day we will meet again
in heaven."

The man was unyielding. Finally Bernardine said: "I am going
to storm heaven for you with a holy violence. While there is still
time, reflect how terrible a thing it is to fall into the hands of the
just Judge of the living and the dead."

St. Bernardine returned to the College and offered Mass for
the man's conversion. Before the Mass was finished the man cried
out: "Father Realino, Father Realino! I want to make peace with
my Creator. I am ready to make a good confession—only deliver
me from the devils that surround me!"

To all sorts and qualities of humanity he was the great teacher
of Lecce. Complicated problems in law or morals were submitted
to his judgment, many of them in the sheaf of letters that the
post brought to him each week. The Archbishop of Otranto came
to consult him, and the Bishop of Oria declared that he set as
much account by Realino's judgments as by those of Sacred
Scripture—a handsome compliment surely. Donato Sacco, a canon
of the Cathedral of Lecce, testifies, "When problems arose in the
Bishop's office in Lecce in regard to faith, superstition and similar
matters, the Bishop as well as his vicars sent me many times to
Father Bernardine to ask his opinion; and their decision never
varied from that of Father Bernardine on points of belief and
practice."

At Naples he had given much of his time to the direction of
young people, especially the students in the Jesuit College. At
Lecce, a number of girls and boys came to him for guidance. He
had the great joy of seeing some of them become priests and religious, and all of them caught in the slow ground swell of re-
newed religious observance that had been set in motion in Lecce.
"Here every Sunday seems a little Easter," he wrote to his brother,
"so many men, women and children receive the Sacraments: God
be praised!"

As in Ars in the nineteenth century, Lecce's renascence of fervor was the flowering of one man's sanctity in the cobbled squares

of a chosen city. "It was because the saints were absorbed in God," says Thomas Merton, "that they were truly capable of seeing and appreciating created things and it was because they loved Him alone that they alone loved everybody." This fact will not appeal to those who believe that sanctity is a kind of dilettantism that does not concern itself with the soiled hands and the empty purses of the poor. Unless we realize the magnitude of the social fact of sanctifying grace, we cannot understand how deeply the saints are involved in the social context of their times. Even those saints who do not go about among their fellowmen but are engaged in contemplating God by prayer and spiritual reading and silent labor in the fields—even these, perhaps these especially—carry out the mission of sanctity: to bring men into the just republic of God's will.

The ancient spiritual writers insisted that those engaged in the ministry take care that their apostolic works be like water overflowing from the brimmed basin of a fountain. If an intense inward union with God is lacking, His interests will be badly served, even though the body is wearied by much scurrying about on what appear to be God's affairs.

The depths to which the saints go in self-abasement is a matter of astonishment to hard-headed men of the world, who can at best presume that these holy men were not insincere. The man of God, with his clearer vision of the divine Majesty, realizes sharply the beggarliness of human nature and the wretched effrontery of sin. Here are some of the notes which Bernardine made on a meditation on humility:

It was borne in upon me that I am nothing and consequently am all sin because sin is nothing. If I am nothing, then there is no point in my grieving if I am not respected, if things are not to my liking, etc. Consequently I owe everything to God Who preserves in me what He has given, because it is His; and the end for which He has given it is His praise and glory. . . .

It was from nothing that God first created light, so if I shall be nothing He will create in me the light of His knowledge, the light of His love, the light to see what is His will.

If I am nothing, I cannot do the least thing, and if I do anything, God does it in me: to Him then be the honor.

Only in a soul with convictions of this sort is there much room, so to say, for God. As the illusions of one's own importance are rooted up and calculations of personal aggrandizement give place to the sowing of God's desires, the clean wheat of zeal and compassion grow up to the harvest. Bernardine's long looks at God and then at himself issued in the life utterly at the service of the people around him and in a power of intercession that again and again worked miracles.

In spite of the fame of his sanctity and the tedious demands of his apostolate, he would not allow himself to seek any exemption from the ordinary life lived by the other Jesuits in the College, and when he could he diminished whatever comfort there was available in his spartan existence. Besides observing all the fasts of the Church even when old age had exempted him, he fasted three days before the feasts of the Blessed Virgin and of his patron saints, and since there were so many of these, he was fasting about three days a week. Even on days when he was not fasting his fare was meager enough: one of his contemporaries estimated it at six ounces of food a day, and an early biographer says that he had given up meat, fish and eggs. At table he would use his knife and fork as busily as anyone, though he ate hardly anything. It was a camouflage used also by St. Robert Bellarmine.

His clothes were ancient and patched, and only Bellarmine, during the provincial visitation, succeeded in getting him to wear a new cassock. His room was poorly furnished, with a rickety lamp and a small table; there were no sheets on the bed, for Bernardine slept in his clothes except when he was ill. Yet he was careful of personal cleanliness and a great admirer of soap and water in a day when these commodities were not at the peak of their popularity. He kept his hair and beard trimmed short, though anyone at all would do for the rôle of barber. Once an amateur badly slashed his ear with the scissors, and Bernardine sat imperturbably while the confused barber stanched the blood with a towel. For another haircut he called in a brother who protested that he knew nothing about haircutting.

"Nonsense," Bernardine said, "the brothers of the Society should know how to do all these things."

When he looked at the results in the mirror there was a long

moment of silence while Father Bernardine surveyed the hum-
mocks of hair and the clearings in between.

"You were right, Brother," he said, "you don't know how to
cut hair. This is enough for now."

We have not much information on the corporal penance he inflicted on himself. The Jesuits who lived in rooms near his could
hear him scourging himself at night, and once someone who came
into his room unexpectedly, discovered that he wore a hairshirt
bristling with iron points. His greatest penance was his availa-
bility to the people, and the effort required to continue year after
year a life divided between communion with God and the clamorous needs of souls. In his old age he was usually left to himself
after sundown, but little of the night was devoted to sleep: four
or five hours were enough for him, and he was strongly opposed
to sleep during the day. As long as he could hobble about his
room, he would not allow anyone else to sweep the floor or arrange the bed. When he was substituting for the absent superior,
he took so much manual labor on himself that the community became alarmed, and old Father Antonio Moresgallo wrote to the
Provincial and was given authority to forbid him to overreach
himself.

Someone told him once that he said, "*Certo*" too frequently,
and he humbly set a watch on what he believed was a manifestation of pride. If he thought he had expressed his opinion too ve-
hemently at a moral theology conference, he would be down on
the floor on his calloused old knees at the next gathering of the
community to ask their pardon. His obedience was the unques-
tioning confidence of a child. Once when the Gesù was being
decorated for a feast day, the more agile of the brethren were
darting up ladders to arrange the hangings of gold and crimson
around the altar. The Rector of the time indulged the whim of
testing the old Saint's obedience. He ordered him to get a ladder
and give a hand in the work. Bernardine immediately slipped off
his cloak, set the ladder in place and was about to climb when the
Rector stopped him with a gesture of satisfaction.

Though he had long since been delivered from the attraction of
carnal sin, he never drew in the sentry lines of modesty and cus-
tody of the senses. The people of Lecce used to remark that if a

lady called on Father Realino at the College, it was hardly worth-
while sitting down because the interview would be over so quickly.
What is less easy to understand is that in his visits to the prisons
he shied away from dealing with the women inmates, though he
encouraged pious women to assist them.

It would be hard to say what devotion held first place in Bernardine's heart. Perhaps it was his love for the Eucharist; to see
him kneeling in prayer before the altar, his hands clasped on his
breast, or if he thought he was alone, outstretched in the form of
a Cross, was to be reminded forcefully of the Presence in the Host.
He came frequently in the day to make visits to the Blessed Sacrament, exhorted his people to frequent Communion, and days of
First Communion were his heart's high holiday. One day when a
boy of five named Claudio Ventura had gone up to the altar and
received the Host, his mother brought him in some agitation to
Father Realino's confessional and explained what had happened.
"Would that Bernardine could receive Our Lord as worthily as
Claudio has!" he said, and he knelt to adore Christ within the
child's flesh, and whispered to the boy the prayers of thanksgiv-
ing he should say.

Love of the Blessed Mother of God was a paramount force in
his life and an occasion for some of the supernatural manifestations which occurred at all stages in his life but were more numerous, or at least more susceptible of verification, in his old age.
He had a vivid realization of the companionship of his guardian
angel, and would sometimes pause before entering a room to let
his angel go before him.

He loved St. Francis Xavier and St. Ignatius and had the happiness of seeing them beatified before his death. They were the
molds of his spirituality: they had emerged from surroundings
not unlike his, they had set the world an example of sanctity in
which the inward consecration and uncompromising self-discipline
went cloaked in the linen and broadcloth of humanistic learning
and knightly courtesy and a sweet urbanity that was the opposite
of worldliness. Since his first discovery of the Jesuit way of life
and the realization that God had given him the grace to make it
his own, he had never lost the happiness that had rolled in on him
like a plumed breaker and flung him to his knees with the power

of a bursting sea. He used to say in his old age that he had never had an unhappy day since he entered religious life, and his return for the vast goodness of God was an immaculate loyalty to his obligations as a religious. After his death his confessor, Father Annibale Vitale, declared on oath that in thirty years he had never known him to commit a venial sin or to violate a rule.

In one of his exhortations to his fellow Jesuits Bernardine said:

I am happy to address you, beloved sons, in that loving phrase of St. John: My little children. . . . Little children are always lovable and do not make objections or resistance; even if you slap them or cuff them, they do not murmur, or show any other resentment than to burst into tears; they do not return injury for injury. And with the same tears, see how the father comforts them: calls them, caresses them, holds them in his arms, upon his heart, and kisses them. Such are my dear Jesuits.

In the *Acta Sanctorum* with the other documents relating to the life of St. Aloysius Gonzaga, is found a letter which Bernardine wrote at the age of seventy-eight to Father Virgilio Cepari, the biographer of St. Aloysius:

The very distinguished life of our blessed brother, Aloysius Gonzaga, written with such faithful scholarship by you, Reverend Father, and printed at Rome, arrived here last month—Deo gratias! How much interest waited on its coming! I am obliged to our Reverend Father Rector because he gave the copy to me in my room before the others received it. So I read it at my leisure during the space of a week, and now it is being read in the refectory (according to the praiseworthy custom that obtains in the Society) so that the whole College may share it. I am finding the second reading a very pleasant repeat performance. . . . It was never my lot to have anything to do with Brother Aloysius (because, believe me, I was not worthy of the honor) and I never even set eyes on him. But from the accounts of others, who were on familiar terms with him, there is evidence enough that he was like a beautifully wrought censer set on the altar of the Most High, breathing forth the sweet odor of a sound and perfect virtue. . . . I must confess the confusion I feel in the Lord when I consider how far apart in the arena of virtue are the youth of Aloysius and my old age— I who am now seventy-eight years old and forty-three years in religion. May I not be confounded forever! I beg your help, Reverend Father, in your holy Masses and your prayers to Blessed Aloysius that at long last I may be made worthy of the promises of Our Lord Jesus, through His mercy alone.

As the old man laid down his pen and lifted his eyes to the open window where a great square of blue Italian sky was framed by an arching branch of an olive tree and the pilastered corner of the church he had built, his heart must have quickened to the memory of a yellow-haired schoolboy in Carpi, who had taken Rodomonte Gonzaga as his hero. And how good God was to bring him through the roadways of glamorous company and violent disappointment and searing sacrifice to the glory of brotherhood with a greater Gonzaga.

IT has been God's will," Bernardine wrote to his brother in 1603, "that this city have a good opinion of me during all the years I have been here, which are already about thirty. I came in the year 1574, and the College was founded, which has grown notably with great benefit to souls. *Deo gratias*."

The "good opinion" which Lecce had of its saint was shared widely through southern Italy and beyond. He became an object of pilgrimage and a living relic; people would gladly make a journey of five or six days to see him and to obtain his blessing. Pilgrims en route to the shrine of Santa Maria de Leuca, at the tip of the heel of Italy, would also visit the Lecce Gesù to see the famous Father Realino. Bishops and princes came in the color and protocol of majesty, stopping the narrow street before the College door with a tangle of gilded coaches and impatient horses and shouting grooms and postilions in embroidered tabards. And muleteers and fish peddlers and charcoal burners gathered about him too, confident that he belonged to them as well as to any perfumed marquis whose pedigree went back to Romulus.

Josiah Acquaviva, Duke of Atri, was proud to be allowed to serve the Saint's Mass, and to receive as a souvenir the water in which Bernardine had washed his fingers. The Theatine Saint, Andrew Avellino, spent some time in Lecce, where he was on familiar terms with Bernardine. Later he declared that Father Realino was indeed a friend of God, whose sanctity was distinguished by humility and charity. The two old gentlemen had much in common: Andrew had practiced law before entering the Theatines, and had been a close friend of Charles Borromeo.

When the galleys of Malta or Venice put in at any of the near-by ports, many of the naval officers would make the trip to Lecce to see Bernardine. And once a whole company of imperial troops, who had been stationed at Bari to repel pirate raids, made a wide detour in their journey westward to winter quarters and trudged into Lecce to see the Saint.

With each week's post came requests for prayers or for advice, or for relics, and visitors to Lecce were given commissions to relay petitions of this sort. Paul V said to a Jesuit who was leaving Rome for Lecce, "Recommend me, and the whole Church, to the holy old man, Father Realino." Father Claudio Acquaviva, who spent half his long lifetime as General of the Jesuits, endured more than his share of bickering, intrigue against the Society, and the burden of responsibility for the work of more than ten thousand Jesuits. When he asked Bernardine's opinion on the advisability of his retiring, the Saint encouraged him to remain in office. The German Emperors, Rudolph II and Matthias, Henry IV of France and Catherine de' Medici asked his prayers, as did the Duke of Mantua, the Elector of Bavaria and the Generals of the Theatines and Celestines.

Father Francis Suarez wrote him a long letter from Rome which ends thus:

I humbly beg Your Reverence to obtain for me from God Our Lord complete conformity to His Will, and a peaceful heart in the midst of all the trials of this world, desiring only one thing: the good pleasure of the Divine Majesty. I hope by Your Reverence's prayers to obtain this gift, which alone in this present life is of any value.

Anna Borromeo, sister of St. Charles, sent an ornament for the Gesù in order to receive a letter from him or a promise of prayers. Ranuccio Farnese, Duke of Parma, and Cesare d'Este, Duke of Modena, asked him to compose a prayer to invoke divine aid for them and their people. Cesare's request he was especially pleased to grant, because the Este house had suffered sharp reverses. In 1597 Duke Alfonso II of Ferrara died—the same Alfonso who had interceded in vain for Bernardine after his arraignment in Carpi. Cesare d'Este, a bastard cousin, was heir, but there was a stronger claimant to the dukedom. Clement VIII had decided that now was the proper moment to bring Ferrara, a papal fief, under the immediate authority of the Holy See. Cesare, though he could muster little military resistance, opposed the papal design, and was excommunicated.

It was a sad time for Bernardine. His loyalty to the Holy See was beyond question, yet he had many friends of former days among the Este, and he always considered himself a subject of the reigning Duke, for Carpi was in the territory of Modena, which Cesare still held as an imperial fief. When the decree of excommunication was read in the Gesù, Bernardine attended with the other Jesuits, but when the moment in the somber ceremony was reached at which the clerics cast to the floor the lighted tapers they had been carrying in their hands, Bernardine's candle would not go out until someone stooped and helped him to extinguish it. Not long afterwards Cesare made peace with the Holy See. When the news was brought to Father Realino, he said simply, "Hearing this is a gift of God."

In answer to the request of the Dukes, Bernardine composed a prayer by combining two orations from the Missal:

Oh God, Whose hand scattereth all good things, grant, I beg, at the prayer of Thy servant, unworthy as I am, that under Thy inspiration and governance I may always do Thy will in thought and deed, and that Thy children, whom in Thy goodness Thou hast committed to me to be guided in the path of peace and justice, may love what Thou hast commanded and desire what Thou hast promised; and so amid the empty follies of the world our hearts may abide where alone we find our true happiness, to the praise and glory of thy most holy Name. Through Christ Our Lord. Amen.

In 1604 a surprising message from Bellarmine, then Archbishop of Capua, brought this reply from Bernardine:

On the vigil of the glorious St. Andrew, our good Father Annibale Vitale arrived, much cheered by his journey, and in particular by his stay with Your Illustrious Lordship, and your most considerate treatment of him. Praise to the divine goodness! He gave me your affectionate remembrances, for which I thank your kind heart, and he said you had commanded him under no circumstances to neglect to tell me three things: first, that you would willingly change places with me; second, that you ask me to tell you by letter whether you are in the grace of God Our Lord; the third, whether you will die in the grace of God. And he said that you repeated these points many times.

I am indeed edified by your genuine humility and candid simplicity, which obliges me to reply as I do, with all sincerity, having recommended the matter many times to Jesus, our sweet Redeemer.

On the first point, I certainly believe you, and because I do, I do not cease to commend you daily to the divine protection.

On the second and third points: I have no doubt that you are in the state of grace, and that, as it has pleased God to place you in the Sacred College, so it will be His pleasure that you die in grace and with much benefit to the souls you govern. The Lord be with you, dearest Father.

I take this opportunity to send you my cordial respects, recommending my old age (I am seventy-four) to your holy sacrifices and prayers so that death will not overtake me in my ingratitude for so many benefits which I know have come to me as a member of this least Society.

Though Bernardine was eager to be of use to everyone, he was troubled by the marks of veneration he received from the powerful and highly placed. When Niccolò Sfondrato had become Gregory XIV in 1590, Giambattista had urged his brother to get in touch with his old friend. Bernardine refused, saying he had long ago given up the pomp and grandeur of courts.

From the moment of his election, which he greeted with honest tears, Gregory felt his incapacity for the papal office. Yet the Cardinals could have chosen many less fitted than this amiable, devout man, a close friend of the charming St. Philip Neri. Whatever may have been the wisdom of Gregory's military campaign against Henry IV of France, he set out a number of wise measures for the good of the Church. He forbade gambling on papal elections, and struck with the sword of excommunication against slavery in the Philippines. He laid the Jesuits forever in his debt by confirming the name "Society of Jesus," which had been called in question by Sixtus V. As he lay dying, the doctors "preserving his life" by administering a potion of powdered gold and gems, he begged the Cardinals to allow him to resign, but without avail. After only ten months in the papal chair he went to join Borromeo, his old tennis partner, whose obsequies he had conducted seven years before.

Bernardine's humility offers a formidable barrier to a full account of the supernatural manifestations which are as important and valid a part of his life as the years at Bologna or his labors in the confessional. We will never know until the reveille of Judgment Day how many visions brought heaven for a while into the cold, bare room of the Saint of Lecce, but some facts are available. There are reliable witnesses, and some of Bernardine's intimates asked him the questions we would like to ask, and we know his answers.

In the documents of the judicial processes which assembled sworn testimonies to Bernardine's sanctity there are many evidences of apparitions of the Blessed Virgin Mary, and this seems to have been the most frequent vision. One of these experiences Bernardine described to a Father Metello Carraciolo, who preached a course of sermons at the Gesù during one Lent. Carraciolo would visit Father Realino each night under the pretext of being of some help to him, for Bernardine was then unwell, but in reality to find out what the Saint was doing. Almost always he found him saying the rosary, and Bernardine was eager to talk about Our Lady. Father Carraciolo bided his time and one night casually asked Father Bernardine—in confidence, of course—whether he had ever seen Mary with the eyes of the body. Bernardine replied candidly that he had; that the Blessed Virgin had appeared to him and talked with him for about a quarter hour.

A nobleman from Bari named Tobia da Ponte was witness of another remarkable incident. He had come to the College to visit Father Realino; unannounced he sat on a bench near the Saint's room to await an opportunity to see him. The corridor was dimly lighted, and the Saint's door was ajar. Da Ponte was surprised to see bright gleams of light coming under the door, as if the room were full of fire. He approached the doorway and saw Bernardine in a kneeling posture some distance above the ground. His arms were extended, there were tears on his face, and again and again he said with great tenderness, "*Gesù, Maria, state in mia compagnia!*" "Jesus, Mary, do not leave me!" Da Ponte watched the spectacle for "about the time it would take to say the Hail Mary slowly," and then returned frightened to the bench. But in a moment he was back at the door, and the scene was unchanged.

At the hearing at which this evidence was recorded, da Ponte could not be shaken in his testimony.

The thing was so clear, beyond doubt and real [he said] that not only did it seem present to me, but I was as certain of it as I am certain of speaking at this moment, and of seeing the things that really are before me. Hence I am sure that it was not imaginary or an illusion, because one, two, three and four times I saw come out, to the width of the door, those glows, lights or rays. . . . I rather began to wonder how there could be a fire in the room, since those rays or sparks came out as if they were caused by a fire inside, exactly as when the blacksmiths strike the hot iron on the anvil; and I got up from the seat on purpose and through the open door I saw with my own eyes Father Bernardine raised up as truly as I see at this moment Your Illustrious Lordship.

It was remarked at times that Bernardine's face shone with light as if the pale flesh and the brittle bone were an alabaster lamp. In his early days in Lecce, something of the sort had been noted. Several members of a family were walking home at night through the darkened streets when their lantern went out for lack of oil. They were near the Church of the Annunziata, which was lighted up as if for a sermon. When they came into the church to beg a little oil, there was no one there but Bernardine absorbed in his prayer, and no lights whatever—not even the sanctuary lamp, for the Blessed Sacrament was not reserved there.

Christmas Eve of 1598 was the occasion for another of the major visions of the Mother and Child. Father Realino sat imprisoned in his confessional, while the traffic of repentance advanced on either side of him, dim shadows through the screen that whispered and bowed their heads to his absolution and then were gone. One of the penitents was his friend Donna Isabella Ventura. She noticed that Bernardine was shaking with cold, and when he had absolved her she went across the nave, a *matrona potens* in full career, and accosted the Rector, Father Alessandro Ferrari, as he sat in his confessional. Father Bernardine was trembling with the cold, and for the love of God would he order him to go to his room and have someone bring him a little fire so that he could warm himself?

The Rector complied immediately, sending Bernardine to his room and asking a lay brother to fetch some of the hot coals from the kitchen hearth. Bernardine meanwhile, kneeling in the chilly room, was quickly lost in the contemplation of the mystery of Christ's birth. The shadowy reasoning of his own prayer gave place to the shining verity of vision: he heard the angels singing and he saw the Virgin Mother, with the Infant on her heart.

"Bernardine, why are you trembling?" Mary asked.

"I'm trembling with the cold," he said, and then Mary placed the Child in his arms. Bernardine embraced Him, and when Mary stooped to take Him back, he asked to hold the Child a little longer.

The brother came laboring up the stairs with the hod of red coals, but hearing the unearthly music and seeing the bright light, he ran to call the Rector. When they had reached the room, the vision was over.

There are more recorded instances, and more witnesses, of the supernatural gifts granted Bernardine in favor of others. The Bollandists, those hard-headed investigators of saintly reputations, call him *"notae sanctitatis thaumaturgus"*—"a famous saint and miracle worker." The various processes list one hundred and seventy-four predictions of the future, twenty-seven instances in which Bernardine seemed to read the secrets of consciences, and seventy-three acts which required superhuman intervention. These numbers represent only those occurrences which came to the attention of the boards of inquiry; there must have been many more. It was a common saying in Lecce that the miracle was the day that passed without a miracle.

The miracle of the wine barrel which was noted soon after Bernardine's coming to Lecce was repeated many years later when the last barrel left in the Jesuits' cellar continued to give wine long after it should have been empty. And one day when there was no bread in the house, Bernardine insisted that the community would assemble at dinner-time as usual. Just as they were gathering, a large gift of fresh bread was brought to the College door.

Predictions of the future were made in detail, and sometimes in defiance of all natural prospects. It was a strange warning that Bernardine gave Giambattista d'Azzia, Marquis of Terza. The Marquis, in perfect health, came with other nobles to call on Father Realino. In the course of their visit, Bernardine took the Marquis aside and said, "My Lord Marquis, the Lord God is giving you today through my lips a salutary warning. In two months, on the Feast of St. Mary Magdalen, you will die. So set your conscience in order and prepare for the long journey to eternity." The Marquis died on the day predicted.

Bernardine assured Don Giulio Acquaviva, who was charged with the defense of the coast of Otranto against the Turks, that there would be no pirate raids for a long time, and so it turned out. Young Vincenzo Caraffa was encouraged, in spite of opposition, to enter the Jesuits, and Bernardine predicted that he would be a devout religious. Caraffa became the seventh General of the Jesuits.

News came one day that two Capuchins, en route to Venice, had been captured by Turkish pirates; the generous Lecceans immediately started a public subscription to pay their ransom. Bernardine, who loved the Capuchins dearly, was happy to give the assurance that while the ship had been boarded by the Turks, the friars and some of the seamen had escaped in the long boat.

A Spanish officer, Didaco Partescia, was assured that a royal warrant was on the way appointing him governor of one of the provinces of the Kingdom of Naples. Three months later he assumed the office. It was no wonder that the Lecceans began to call their Saint "The Angel of Good News."

In regard to this charism of prophecy, Father Francesco Mirabelli declared in his sworn deposition, "The gift of prophecy which, to my own personal knowledge, Father Bernardine exercised, was of a kind that you could hardly read of in the lives of other saints, because it was almost continual and in many cases descended to minute particulars."

Bernardine's cures were worked simply; they followed hours of prayer, as all his external acts were islanded in a vast sea of prayer, or were accomplished by asking the sick person to say a brief prayer with him, and then laying his hands on the suppliant's head or blessing him. Sometimes in his latter years he used relics of St. Irene in his cures. This was not the St. Irene, the virgin martyr of Salonika, who was one of the patrons of Lecce, but another, evidently martyred at Rome. The *cultus* of the two saints caused some confusion and some acrimonious exchanges between the Jesuits, who possessed the relics of St. Irene of Rome, and the Theatines, whose church in Lecce was dedicated to the other

Irene. Eventually Paul V confirmed the Jesuits in their possession of the relics, but stipulated that they must celebrate the feast of their Irene on a different day from the one which the Theatines devoted to the city's patron.

The St. Irene whom Bernardine invoked must not be thought of as a kind of celestial Mrs. 'Arris, a pious deception adopted for humility's sake to hide Bernardine's own powers. He attributed to her his own cure from a skin disease which he had borne for four years, and recorded the cure in a poem which he attached to the shrine of the martyr in a simple gesture of gratitude:

I testify that for four years a disease known only by myself afflicted me, raising a scurf on my flesh;
But lately, when the bones of Blessed Irene gave forth a heavenly perfume, and I raised my voice to praise this marvel,
Lo, the unclean blight left me, though I took no medicine, and my skin became clean again like the skin of a child.
Holy maid Irene, it was you who saw all my plight and worked this cure. And would it not be unjust to be silent about the truth?

When a silver statue of the little Saint was set in place in the Gesù, her relics were carried in a solemn procession. Old and stooped as he was, Bernardine insisted that he be one of the four to carry the canopy over the relics. A friend in Naples, Father Mario d'Andria, expressed his surprise at Bernardine's agility, in a little verse, and Bernardine replied in the following verses:

> Why should it smack of marvel, dear old friend,
> That I, an old man, bore the royal veil
> Above the blessed bones of dear Irene?
> A sweet strength from on high sustains us yet
> And rules us, arm and foot and cunning hand.
> An old man speaks the truth: 'Tis Irene's work;
> The lion-lamb still shares her martyr's power.

From the thronging miracles of Bernardine's latter years, we will dwell on only four, and let them stand typical for the rest.

The Baroness of San Cesare, who lived in a castle three miles from Lecce, had sent to Father Bernardine asking for prayers in her illness and for some blessed object. The Saint sent her a bottle of holy water and gave the assurance that she had nothing to fear.

Meanwhile her fever increased and the physicians gave up hope for her recovery. Her confessor, Father Annibale Vitale, was sent for, to hear her confession and give her Holy Viaticum. As Vitale left the College, Bernardine again declared that the Baroness had nothing to fear. On his return, Father Vitale reported that Her Ladyship had only a few hours to live.

"Oh, no!" Bernardine exclaimed. "She will certainly be cured."

The carriage from the castle was at the College the next day, and Father Vitale was fetched post-haste to anoint the Baroness, who had grown worse in the night. He repeated Bernardine's assurance, which the relatives received with disbelief: the old Saint was obviously mistaken. This seemed to be the fact of the matter, for the Baroness stopped breathing and the body became cold. The great bell in the castle tower tolled to announce the death, and preparations were begun for the funeral. Some of the servant maids were washing the body when they noticed a slight movement of the head. The body was brought back to the bed, and the noble lady soon opened her eyes, and, the chronicle continues, demanded a drink. There was no doubt of her recovery, and soon she was able to come to Lecce to say her thanks to Father Bernardine.

A nobleman named Giovanni Caputo, from Carovigno, near Brindisi, came to the College to ask Bernardine to pray that God would give him a son. His three boys had been carried off by sickness, and the only surviving child was a girl of seven months. The nobleman was bidden to dinner with the Jesuits, and was about to enter the refectory when news came from Carovigno: his child was desperately ill. Bernardine wept, and knelt with the distracted father and said the Litany of the Blessed Virgin.

Caputo flung himself on his horse and galloped homeward. Two days later, a courier brought a message asking the Saint to redouble his prayers, for the doctors could give no hope for recovery. Bernardine wrote a reply to Caputo, and the messenger folded it in his belt and was off in a reckless spatter of hoofbeats. Giovanni took heart when he read the note in Bernardine's clear, strong script: "Be of good courage: God will give your child back her health and make her His servant on earth and His angel in heaven." The baby seemed at the point of death, but when the father tucked the note from the Saint into her clothing, she fell asleep. She slept soundly for eight hours, the breathing becoming easier and the color of rosebuds returning to her face. Many years later she became a nun, fulfilling the second part of the prediction.

If it seems that many of Father Realino's miracles were brought to pass in favor of the nobility (for the biographers seem to prefer such instances), we must not overlook Betta, a little girl of six or seven, whose cure must have been a particularly happy one for the Saint. Betta, whose father was a baker, was playing near the fire when she was struck in the right eye by a burning coal. Her screams brought her mother running from the bakery counter, but it was too late: according to sworn testimony given later, the eyeball was completely destroyed. Bernardine's friend, Donna Isabella Ventura, brought Betta to the College to beg the Saint's help; Bernardine and Betta knelt together and said the Hail Mary, the child repeating it after him, because she did not know the prayer. Then Bernardine applied a relic of St. Irene, sprinkled the little girl with holy water and blessed her. As yet there was no sign of a cure.

Late that night there was a frantic knocking at the Ventura door, and Donna Isabella recognized the voice of the baker's wife calling her name. Betta was cured, the burned flesh was sound and the eye restored.

There were various other cures of blindness, one performed in favor of Filippo Cardinal Spinelli, brother of Father Provincial Spinelli. At another time, a priest, Orazio Teofilatto, blinded by a disease which had attacked both eyeballs, was led to the Jesuit house and to the bedside of the Saint, who was lying sick himself. Bernardine asked Orazio to kneel beside the bed, and he traced a sign of the Cross on his eyes. Immediately Teofilatto began to see, gray indistinct shapes at first, then clearly with restored vision.

Wonders of this sort, especially those that were worked at a distance with only some object blessed by Bernardine, or that he had used, caused a frantic hunt for relics of the Saint. Father Marcello de Prato, Provincial of the Capuchins, asserted in the pulpit the miraculous power of the relics, but this assurance was not needed: too many marvels had been attributed already to letters written by Realino, or to the touch of the long staff he used. The pious larceny went beyond all bounds, and the Rector of the College offered to put a lock on Bernardine's door to stop the thievery, but the Saint declined, even though his own brethren had sometimes joined in this grotesque discourtesy. Once when he was saying Mass, another priest appropriated his skull-cap, but gave it back when he saw the look of pain on Bernardine's face. Even Father Muzio Vitelleschi, then Provincial of Naples and later to be General, joined the hunt. At the community recreation he reproached the Rector because Father Realino's staff was in such poor condition; the wood had cracked and had been clumsily mended. A new staff was provided, and Vitelleschi had his relic.

The widespread report that letters written by the Saint had worked cures caused every scrap of his handwriting to be devoutly prized. Germier says that Brother Soria became *"un vero tiranno"* in the matter of inducing him to write *"biglietti di sanità"* —"health notes"—for various sufferers. They were slips of paper on which Bernardine had written some short prayer. Once when instance was made to Giulio Mastrilli, Imperial Commissioner in Lecce, for the release of a prisoner, he asked for a written recommendation from Father Realino. The Saint knew that it was an attempt to obtain a relic, and dictated the recommendation; though Mastrilli insisted that the letter be in Bernardine's hand he refused to comply.

There was little he could do to discourage the adulation that surrounded him. If it could not be passed over in silence he rebuked it with a grief that came from the depths of his heart. Once when he was vice-rector he imposed a penance on one of the Jesuits who called him Saint—for abusing a title so sacred. A lawyer was guilty of the same gaucherie, and Bernardine said quickly, "A fine saint indeed! Bernardine, the world's worst sinner, is canonized by a snap of the fingers. Sir, your standards must be quite low if you think Bernardine is a saint." A certain Marchioness d'Oria, who had been too outspoken in her veneration of his sanctity, never found him at home when she called at the College thereafter. He was honestly astounded that he should be taken for an oracle and miracle-worker, and the folly of those who praised his holiness or went on their knees to kiss the hem of his cassock embarrassed him to tears.

Father Bernardo Colnago, whose cause has been introduced for canonization, came down from Bari one day to see him. When he kissed the hem of Bernardine's cassock, the old Saint exclaimed, "Do you go through these useless ceremonies too? You are Bernardo and I am Bernardine, the lesser Bernard. It is for me, as the inferior, to show deference to you."

This tactless veneration of a city in love with a saint was the only cloud upon his days as the shadows deepened in the long evening of his life, and he spoke of going home.

ALL the extant portraits of Father Realino show the wrinkled face and white hair of old age. "The holy old man" was a phrase that came naturally with his name, for he had begun to look an old man at fifty, and he lived out the gracious span of eighty-five years. In the choir of canonized Jesuits only one is older than he: St. Alphonsus Rodriguez, who was born and died within a year of St. Bernardine's birth and death.

At fifty-seven Realino was described in the catalogue of the Jesuits of the Neapolitan Province as "of declining strength," and ten years later he was listed among the *seniles*. Yet in his mid-seventies he was still in "middling good health," as he wrote to Giambattista:

To tell the truth, at the rate I'm going I'm afraid I'll be able to live some years more, since I have all the powers I need, namely a clear head, a good stomach, good eyesight and hearing. I read without spectacles, write with a firm and not a trembling hand, I can stay many hours in the confessional without getting exhausted, and I can do a little other work besides, but in all my activity there are some signs of old age. My legs are tired, so I never go out any more unless it is in a carriage if at any time some sick person calls me to hear his confession or to settle a case of conscience.

In 1607, consequent on the failure of the harvests, famine struck large areas of Italy. To Bernardine, the desperate need of his people, the cries of the hungry besieging the College for help, were a personal challenge, a bugle blowing the last charge. He was seventy-seven, a bent old man leaning on a staff, hardly able to stir beyond the College door, and still the comfort of his love went out to every corner of the city. He would leave untouched the delicacies that rich friends sent for his own dinner, but he begged large sums of money and spent it with his old prodigality for bread and soup and wine for the poor. We can only regret that so few details of this famine year have been preserved by the Saint's biographers; there must have been incidents to rival the *Fioretti* in this last feeding of the multitude.

As he approached his eightieth birthday, his strength had failed so much that sometimes his stiff old legs gave out and he fell; at least once he collapsed in the confessional. There was some doubt whether he would be able to say Mass on his eightieth Christmas, for often even this effort was too much for him; he made the attempt, and actually said the three Christmas Masses, standing at the altar for nearly two hours with no apparent difficulty.

On the morning of March 3, 1610, he was hearing confessions as usual in the Church. When a penitent asked him for some pious object—a medal or a rosary—he arose, kissed his stole and hung it on its hook, and went slowly, his staff tapping on the stone, across the nave and through the sacristy, along the corridor and up the stone steps to his room. As he was returning he missed his footing at the top of the staircase and pitched down the flight of steps. When they found him he was lying insensible, his head on the stone floor, and the blood flowing from gashes in his chin and over his left eye. He was carried into a room on the ground floor, next to the sacristy, and this was to be his room during the last six years of his life. For two hours he was unconscious, and the report spread in the city that he was at the point of death. Eager for the most precious relic of all, the people wiped up every drop of the blood that lay in a dark stain at the foot of the staircase, and some of the hardier ones profited by the confusion to go up to his room and tear his manuscripts into pieces and break up his long staff. The viceroy came to offer his sympathy and was given the needle which had been used to close the wounds, and part of the bandage.

Little by little the doctors brought him around, but the fall seemed to have shattered the Saint's fragile strength. His injuries healed badly and when the surgeon hesitated to use his knife for fear of further disfigurement, Bernardine urged him to do what was necessary without regard to the appearance of his face. It was nearly two months before he was able to leave his bed, but through all his sufferings his serenity never grew less. He mentioned his injuries in a letter to his nephew, and added:

Dear Jesus has been pleased to console me in this heavy cross, and
I can truly say that the misfortune has been a blessing to me, because
I had constantly before my mind the passion of Our Lord, and the sins
of my youth, and many times I confessed them; so that in the more
than fifty days that I was abed I was always in consolation of spirit.

Bernardine's association of his sufferings with the passion of
Jesus was ratified by Christ Himself. There are two apparitions
reported; one, in the night of March 24th, was a vision of Christ
crucified, and Father Antonio Beatillo, in his sworn deposition,
declared that at this time Christ revealed to the Saint certain mysteries of the Faith. In a later vision, Bernardine saw Jesus crowned
with the thorn garland of His mock kingship. The Savior took one
of the thorns and pressed it into Bernardine's head, but the point
of the thorn remained in the Head of Christ. This mystical experience gave no pain, and the Saint begged Christ to prolong the
illness, because it was the occasion of so many favors.

Father Beatillo and three other priests gave the same account of
this vision, as well as Brother Giuseppe Soria. And, oddly enough,
Bernardine recorded the vision in two poems, one of which he
dictated the day after the first vision, on the morning of March
24th, the other evidently written the following month. Both compositions, though hardly of literary merit (it would be graceless
to ask for that also), are lively evidences of the sharpness of the
Saint's mental powers in his old age. The first, written in Italian,
is a sonnet; the second is in simple Latin distichs:

> A thorn is lodged in my brow, but it has no barb
> The barb you save for yourself, oh Christ!
>
> Such floods of peace wash over me, darling Lord,
> When I in my weakness think on your holy wounds:
>
> Prolong the days of these present ills, I pray,
> And tarry the longer with me in my joy.

To this verse Bernardine himself gave the title: "Lines of an
eighty-year-old religious of the Society of Jesus, seriously ill during March and April, 1610."

Eventually he was able to offer Mass again, until about 1613, when weakness and failing vision deprived him of this consolation. Even then he was not cast down: he received Holy Communion daily and said his beads almost constantly, and declared that he was happy to live like a Jesuit brother, as he had desired to do when he was a novice. He did not resume his old post in the confessional, but until the day of his death he heard the confessions of men in his room. From his ground-floor room he could hobble the few steps across the sacristy and sit lost in contemplation before the altar until the shadows gathered in the corners of the church and the failing sun made a mellow glory in the clerestory windows.

There was another vision of the Mother and Child about this time, and it is recorded in the simple narrative of Brother Soria, who gave the following testimony in the canonization inquiries:

Having the duty in our College of going about to light the lamps in the rooms of the Fathers, in the morning at the hour of rising, I came one morning to light the lamp in the room of the said Father Bernardine. This Father, with a very joyful face, in a jubilant voice said to me: "Close the door, Brother Gioseffo, because I want to tell you some good news. The *Madonna Santissima* has been here and I have seen her; and she departed just this moment."

And then I expressed disappointment at not having arrived sooner, and perhaps seen the *Madonna Santissima*, and I told him that I wanted to continue to light the lamps for the other Fathers, and then I would return to His Reverence, so that he might tell me the favors the *Madonna Santissima* had granted him. And when I returned in a short while, the said Father Bernardine told me: That the *Madonna Santissima* had been here, "and she had the *Bambino* in her arms, and she gave Him to me to hold in my arms." And while Father Bernardine said these words to me, he wept with great tenderness, and when I asked him how the *Madonna* had looked, the said Father Bernardine told me that she had appeared in a blue mantle, and that she was very beautiful. And I have always kept this vision in my memory.

Soria went in all haste to tell the news to the Rector, Father Orazio Sabatino. But visions were no novelty now in the College of Lecce. "Father Bernardine is always conversing with the *Madonna* and the angels," Sabatino said. And, indeed, the association of the Saint with Christ and His Mother seemed to be as in-

timate as if he lived in their visible company.[1] His bitter grief at
Jesus' sufferings was noted at a Passion Play given at the College
two years before his death. When Christ's triumph was portrayed
in the final scenes, the tears were dashed away, and the Saint's
face was radiant with joy in His Master's victory.

Like a theme of a symphony, which recurs in the final movement with greater power and meaning and fresh accessions of
beauty, the lovely qualities of Bernardine Realino's life were
never more evident than in his last few years: the gentle speech,
the tender love of his friends, the apostolic compassion that could
discern even in the most stupid slave or the coarsest slum dweller
the secret of God's face. If he offered his sufferings again and
again for "the sins of my youth," so many other scenes crowded
in on his mind to lift up his heart or to beckon him down a teeming street of memory. There was his mother's face, and the thought
of her would bring the quick tears; the way his father had gone
into the saddle and lifted his gloved hand in farewell as he rode
off to Mantua or Trent; the masquers and the tumblers and the
riot of the fiddles and the drums at the Modena carnival; Chloris,
and the long, aching hours at the legal texts; the flash of a sword
at Carpi, and the color and solemnity of his *doctoratio;* the pain
and loneliness at Cassine and then the total sacrifice in the open
gateway of success. They were not really distractions, because he
made them premises for prayer and begged God not to assess with
too sharp an eye the stewardship of all the good things that had
been given him.

He became gradually weaker and was quite dependent on the
care of the faithful brother. Still the labor of confession went on,
and though he was half-blind, and it seemed at times that age was
dimming his memory, in hearing confessions he had not lost any
of his old brilliance. ·

The report of his decline went out on all the wings of rumor.
Lecce sensed the pulse of history that throbbed through these
memorable days; the people were anxious that every detail of the

---

[1] Some of Realino's biographers assert that the Saint admitted to his
Provincial, Father Antonio Spinelli, that he had continually a corporal vision
of the Blessed Virgin, which seems inconsistent with the accounts of individual visions.

idyll of Bernardine's life among them should be recorded and made available to the Church as evidence for canonization. And when his tired hand could no longer be lifted to absolve and bless, they hoped that still he would be their protector: as in the whole of life, so also and much more in death.

The matter was broached in the city council on December 21, 1615, and the Mayor of Lecce offered a remarkable resolve of which the sense at least has been preserved:

GENTLEMEN: Since, by a particular favor of God, for more than forty years our city has had in its midst the theologian and priest of the Society of Jesus, Father Realino, who has always edified us by the extraordinary sanctity of his life, and by the abundant blessings which, as everyone knows, he has received continually and still receives each day from the blessed God,—the favor of so many prophecies and miracles that there is hardly a single person not only in this city and district, but even in a large part of this province and in many other places in the Kingdom, and other, far-off provinces, who has not experienced in himself some of those graces which God Our Lord has given by means of this blessed servant of His;

Whereas, because many of these miracles, prophecies and favors will in time become difficult of proof because of the death of many witnesses (a thing of daily occurrence) and in the hope that one day the said blessed Father Bernardine must surely be glorified by God and become after death the city's heavenly protector, as he protects us now and has for so many years past, during his life on earth, by his holy merits and prayers;

Be it resolved: to make, in the name of this our city, an authoritative petition to our Lord Bishop, that he grant the power to summon witnesses and examine them under oath, and that their testimonies be taken for the sake of every laudable purpose they will serve, and especially with a view to a perpetual record as well as in preparation for his canonization, if it will be God's will to canonize him after his death;

And likewise with the same care to make a similar request in the name of the city to other bishops, prelates and ordinaries of any part of the world where witnesses could be found who would be able to depose as above; and furthermore petition must be made, with the same diligent expenditure of effort, to our Holy Lord, Pope Paul V.

So in the same turbulent little senate where once the Jesuits had been proscribed, the first steps were taken toward Father

Realino's canonization. The canonical processes were not actually instituted until after his death, and the cause advanced slowly, often halted by the troubles of the Church or the falling fortunes of the Jesuits. Leo XIII made him Blessed in 1896, and on June 22, 1947, the long quest, begun in Lecce three hundred years before, came to its triumphant end. For Italy and the world, Pope Pius XII, amid the trumpet echoes of apostolic majesty, proclaimed him St. Bernardine: a moment before the thunder of the *Te Deum* rolled like a great surf through the Vatican Basilica.

In the months of invalidism before his death, the long leisure of the sickroom gave Bernardine the opportunity to set his thoughts in verse, for he had never quite given up poetry. The few of these poems that are extant compensate us in some measure for the loss of the earlier ones. A pleasant little epigram brings an echo of the humanistic ardors of his youth, and links them with his home city and the Saint who had given him his name:

> Carpi, my birthplace, means *fruit* in Greek,
> The fruit of my life I have still to seek;
> An idle farmer, a fertile field:
> Saint of Siena, bless the yield!

His longer poem on Bernardine of Siena, published originally in a life of the Franciscan Saint written by Father Vincenzo Mastareus in 1628, is reprinted in the *Acta Sanctorum*, with the hint that Bernardine wrote it in the year of his death. If this translation reproduces only the *cantabile* quality of the rhythm of the original, that may be sufficient warrant for flouting Belloc's precept that poetry is rarely to be translated into poetry.

> Hail, herald of God's majesty,
> St. Francis' faithful son,
> The angels bless the name you bear
> And the halo you have won.
>
> Your youth you gave to Mary's heart,
> And charmed at love like this,
> She came from heaven to bless your vow
> And offered her hands to kiss.

Siena fed your boyhood years,
At Aquila you died;
Your glory and gentle Celestine's
At Aquila abide.

Your life burned like a tallow torch,
A candle to a star,
For her who goes gowned with the sun
Forever where you are.

Oh, shining too in that far height,
Dear Bernardine, look down
With love on all the fields you knew
And every little town.

And bless me still, sweet father and saint,
Whose name I wear for mine,
And bring me out of the mist and the sea,
Your love like a great cloak sheltering me
Till the harbor cressets shine.

Two other poems written, or more probably dictated, for the old eyes were growing dim, reflect Bernardine's eagerness to cut the last slender tether that bound him to the earth:

Naught less than you, sweet death, can please me now,
Only your footfall sends my sorrows flying;
Come, take me where the deep waters flow,
By the pleasant road to the happy bridge of dying.

The second, which hardly preserves in translation the childlike intensity of the Italian original, is addressed to Christ Our Lord:

Jesus, love of my heart, my peace, my life,
When shall I see you in the streets of heaven?

I melt like a candle starred with that burning hope—
To turn and find you standing at my side.

The lovely thought, so precious to my mind,
Prints on my heart your Face like a die of gold;

And happier run the hours while I read,
Your love my book, your wounds its printed page.

At the beginning of the year 1616, Father Antonio Beatillo said to him, "Dear Father, the new year has begun." Bernardine replied, "Yes, the new year has come and this is the year we shall take our leave."

When his friends, Teofilo and Marcantonio Zimara, came to visit him, he said, "We shall see each other no more in this world; take care of yourselves and your family. I will never forget you, and I will keep you always in my prayers to the Lord." To Brother Soria, who feared that there might be another fall and that he might die unattended, he gave the assurance that he would die in the comfort of the sacraments.

Father Beatillo, who preached the Lenten sermon course in the Gesù that year, was at Rome later in the spring. As he was about to return to Lecce he visited Cardinal Bellarmine to say his farewell. St. Robert, then in his seventy-fourth year, had a message for his old friend. Father Brodrick relates the incident in a passage he quotes from the *Summarium* of Bellarmine's canonization process:

"Father Antonio [the Cardinal said] I want you to do me a favor. When you reach Lecce, tell the holy old man, Father Bernardine Realino, that, as he is now so advanced in years and incapable of doing anything more in this world, he must hasten on to Heaven as fast as he can and prepare a place there for me."

Beatillo recalls how Bernardine received the Cardinal's rather blunt greeting:

Immediately on my arrival in Lecce, I gave the Cardinal's message to Father Bernardine. His answer was: "*Padre mio,* I shall be leaving this world in a few days and I shall carry out my Lord Cardinal's directions. When, by the grace of God, I get to Heaven, I shall be on the lookout for him and have his place ready, and Your Reverence may tell His Lordship this from me."

That was in mid-June, 1616. A few days before, on June 11th, a fever and other symptoms of weakness had caused some alarm, but Bernardine had not asked for the last sacraments. On the morning of the twenty-ninth day of the month he was found to be feverish again and to have lost the use of his speech, though he was quite conscious. There could be no doubt that his end was near, and with much sadness the fathers of the College began the solemn protocol of the death of a saint. His confessor, Father Annibale Vitale, received his confession as well as he could, and they brought him Holy Communion, the flat tinkle of the little bell approaching clearer as if an angel were walking across the stone floor shod in silver sandals. While his fellow Jesuits knelt around the bed, Father Antonio Moresgallo anointed him, and Bernardine closed his eyes and offered his hands as all the portals of the senses were signed with the oil of the sacrament.

The Rector, Father Paolo Torrisio, wished to keep the tragic news a secret within the community but this was an unreal hope. Within a few hours the whole city knew that Father Bernardine was dying, and as the crowd gathered before the College and filled the narrow street, the Jesuits realized that all Lecce was coming to say farewell. The precaution was taken of reinforcing the doors with props and bars, and as the day wore on and the people became more insistent and more noisy, an armed guard was sent for and a platoon of soldiers pushed their way through the yelling mob and took up their station at the portal of the College.

At length Father Rector decided to admit the people to Bernardine's room a few at a time. Some of the priests would be present constantly to attend to the Saint's needs and to keep the files of people in order. They came in for a moment, knelt beside the bed and kissed the dying man's hand or touched him with some religious object. Only men were allowed in the sickroom, women being excluded by the law of cloister.

On the evening of Friday, July 1st, Monsignor Scipione Spina, Bishop of Lecce, who had been kept at home by gout until now, came with the Vicar General. Until that hour, the looting of the room for relics had been sternly prevented by the Jesuits standing guard. What was their dismay to see His Lordship draw a knife and cut off part of the bedclothes. The other Lecceans present needed no other encouragement; in a few moments they had hardly left enough clothing on the bed to cover the dying man, and they seized other furnishings of the room that Bernardine might have used.

This same Lecce mob a few days hence would again almost

strip the Saint in his coffin, and would tear out hair and toenails
for relics, surging around the bier and fighting over their prizes.
The soldiers were unable to cope with the rioters, and the Jesuits
and the canons of the cathedral had to let a few ragged psalms
suffice for the Office of the Dead. The hapless Carmelite who attempted to pronounce the Saint's eulogy gave up in despair. Late
that night, when the soldiers had finally cleared the church with
drawn swords, there was a council of war for the bedraggled Jesuits, the diocesan authorities and the city fathers. Further violence
was feared for the next day, the day set for the funeral, when the
Lecce populace would be reinforced by crowds from the neighboring villages. The possibility was not remote that the people
would use their knives on the dead body. The decision was taken
to proceed immediately to the burial, and so before daybreak
Bernardine was entombed in the church he had built.

Perhaps these scenes of excessive devotion were compensated
for by the delegation that waited on the Saint that memorable
Friday, July 1st, the day before he died. It was the Mayor and the
chief officers of the government, come to beg the final favor in
the name of the city. They gathered around the bed, young lords
in their ruffs and rich Spanish black, gray-bearded councillors old
enough to remember when they had hailed Father Bernardine into
Lecce on a Sunday morning long ago. They went awkwardly on
their knees while the Mayor, Don Sigismondo Rapanà, unrolled a
document and began to read. His address is extant at least in substance, if not verbatim:

Dearest father of all of us: There is no doubt that, to our great grief,
the hour is at hand when you are to leave us. Our desire would be that
for our consolation and help we could remain with you always, but
since God is calling you away to heaven, we commend to your prayers
ourselves and our entire city, which you have loved so well and which
has always held you in the highest reverence. In your great charity,
Father, grant this city what it hopes for: that it will continue to have
you as our defender and protector in heaven, which we now constitute
you from this hour forever. We, your servants and sons, beg your
assent; do not forget us, whose hearts are sore at your departure.

In the tense silence that followed, Bernardine could only sigh,
and the delegation took this as a sign of his consent. But the

Mayor was not satisfied; the matter was of such moment in the city's history that he hoped for a more unequivocal sign of the Saint's acceptance. The delegation returned the following day and Don Sigismondo, standing in the midst of the kneeling councillors, repeated the city's petition. This time a look of paternal tenderness came on the face of the dying man, and he bowed his head and murmured some word that could not be understood. But the magistrates were satisfied that Bernardine had granted their request. They kissed his hand and filed out of the death-room, weeping without shame.

In the early afternoon, the moment of departure seemed near, and Father Antonio Moresgallo read the chief articles of Catholic belief and Bernardine professed his faith in each by laboriously inclining his head. They began the prayers for the dying, which he evidently understood. He lay with his arms crossed on his breast like a Crusader, kissing the crucifix that was often brought to his lips, while the deep waters of prayer poured around him like the tides of eternity coming in.

Fearing that the long prayers of the ritual were tiring him, they urged the dying man to rest, and there were some moments of quiet in the room while Father Realino lay as if asleep. But soon he made a sign that he wished the prayers to go on. He was now in his agony, and as the breath came stertorously, and the shoulders heaved, the brethren around the bed murmured to him the names of Jesus and Mary and Ignatius. His eyes were fixed on the crucifix, and for a moment he recovered his speech and made a final prayer. "*O Madonna mia santissima!*" he said.

Toward four o'clock, the hour of vespers of the Feast of the Visitation of Mary, there was a rustling in Bernardine's throat, and at this portent Father Antonio Beatillo began to read from the Ritual the Passion of Our Lord according to St. John. He had reached the trial of Jesus before Caiphas, and the blow upon the face given by the servant of the high priest, when the dying man was shaken by a slight spasm. Father Beatillo quickly closed the book and placed a lighted candle in St. Bernardine Realino's hand, and bent to whisper the sacred Names. And so, with the candle casting a glory around his head, he lifted his eyes and died.

BIBLIOGRAPHY

H IPPOLYTE DELEHAYE, the Bollandist, had no sanguine view of the ultimate fate of those who presume to write the life of a saint. "Hagiographers, alas," he said, "have sinned greatly, and the only consolation left us is to believe that much will be forgiven them. . . . There is no form of literature into which people rush so frequently without any sort of preparation."

If only to justify myself to the skeptical shade of Father Delehaye I enumerate here the books which have been my chiefest guides in the journey in search of Bernardine Realino and the "enchanted region of the Renaissance" in which he lived. The best life of Bernardine is Father Giuseppe Germier's *San Bernardino Realino* (Florence, Libreria Editrice Fiorentina, 1943) and I have relied most heavily on it for the facts of Bernardine's life and especially for quotations from his writings. If I have departed from Germier's account of an incident it has been only on the evidence of the Saint's own letters or the formidable authority of Father Girolamo Tiraboschi, S.J. Tiraboschi's *Storia della Letteratura Italiana* (Rome, Salvoni, 1797) sketches Bernardine's litterary achievements, and his *Biblioteca Modenese* (Modena, Società Tipografica, 1781–86) contains a lengthy biographical notice of the Saint. Other lives of Bernardine which I have consulted are *Le Bienheureux Bernardin Realino, S.J.,* by R. Bouman, S.J. (Paris, Desclée, 1896); *La Vie Merveilleuse du Bienheureux P. Bernardin Realino, S.J.,* by Eugene Seguin, S.J. (Lyons, E. Vitte, 1896); *Storia della Vita del B. Bernardino Realino* by Ettore Venturi, S.J. (Roma, Brefani, 1895).

Material in English is limited to pamphlets and articles, some of them written with a degree of detachment from the available facts. The best account in English of Bernardine's life is found in a pamphlet, *Blessed Bernardine Realino of the Society of Jesus* (New York, Apostleship of Prayer, 1896), and the best of the articles is a sympathetic study in the English *Letters and Notices* for September, 1947. The notice in the Attwater-Thurston revision of Alban Butler's *Lives of the Saints* (New York, Kenedy) devotes too much space to an account of instances of blood-liquefaction associated with the body of the Saint, which phenomena have now ceased; and for the Saint's name, the form *Rea-*

lini is used, which the researches of Tiraboschi in the Saint's own letters proved incorrect.

St. Bernardine's book, *In Nuptias Pelei et Tethydis Catullianas Commentarius* (Bologna, Giaccarelli, 1551) was made available on microfilm by the University of Chicago Library and Butrigarius' *Quaestiones Legales* (Bologna, Giaccarelli, 1557), for which Bernardine wrote an introductory poem, I used at the Harvard Law School Library. The first edition of Gruter's *Lampas, sive Fax Artium Liberalium . . . Thesaurus Criticus* (Frankfort, 1602–1634) contains the *Adnotationes* published originally with the Catullan commentary; it seems to have been omitted in later editions of the *Thesaurus Criticus*.

Throughout the biography valuable help was found in *The Civilization of the Renaissance in Italy* by Jakob Burckhardt (New York, Boni, 1935); the *Jesuiten-lexikon,* edited by Ludwig Koch (Paderborn, Verlag Bonifacius-druckerei, 1934); *The Jesuit Code of Liberal Education* by Allan P. Farrell, S.J. (Milwaukee, Bruce, 1938); and the *Enciclopedia Italiana* (Rome, Istituto della Enciclopedia Italiana, 1929–1937), notably in the articles on Alberto Pio, Ludovico Castelvetro, and the Davalos family.

Other books were consulted for particular chapters:

Chapter One. The material on the life of Rodomonte Gonzaga was found in the following: Christopher Hare's life of Rodomonte's sister, Giulia Gonzaga, *A Protestant Princess of the Italian Reformation* (New York, Scribner's); *The Vocation of Aloysius Gonzaga* by C. C. Martindale, S.J. (London, Sheed and Ward, 1929); *Memoirs of Benvenuto Cellini* (New York, National Library, 1900); *The History of the Popes* by Ludwig von Pastor, volumes 9–10 (St. Louis, Herder, 1898).

Chapters Two and Three. The edition of Fynes Moryson's *Itinerary* used is J. Maclehose's, Glasgow, 1907. The material on the University of Bologna was found in *The Universities of Europe in the Middle Ages* by Hastings Rashdall, M.A. (Oxford, the Clarendon Press, 1936); *Life in the Medieval University* by Robert S. Rait (Cambridge, the University Press, 1912); *Histoire des Universités Françaises et étrangères* (Paris, Picard, 1933). The history of the academies was illuminated by Thomas F. Crane's *Italian Social Customs of the Sixteenth Century* (New Haven, Yale University Press, 1920).

Chapter Four. The history of the Spanish overlordship in Milan and the sequences of governors are given in volume XIII of the *Cambridge Modern History* (New York, Macmillan, 1902–1912). The life of St. Charles Borromeo used is Margaret Yeo's *Reformer, St. Charles Borromeo* (Milwaukee, Bruce, 1938).

Chapter Six. Edward Hutton's *Naples and Southern Italy* (New York, Macmillan, 1924) and Martin Shaw Briggs' *In the Heel of Italy* (London, Melrose, 1910) were invaluable for their impressions of Lecce and the Apulian countryside.

Chapter Eight. The history of baroque architecture is adequately summarized in *A History of Architecture* by Fiske Kimball and G. H. Edgell (New York, Scribner's, 1918).

Chapter Ten. References to Bellarmine in this and the thirteenth chapter are taken from *The Life and Works of Blessed Robert Bellarmine, S.J.*, by James Brodrick, S.J. (New York, Kenedy, 1928). The life of Blessed Charles Spinola used is *A Prisoner in Japan* by D. Donnelly, S.J. (London, Sheed and Ward, 1928).

Chapters Eleven and Thirteen. The letter on St. Aloysius Gonzaga and the poem on St. Bernardine of Siena are found in the May and June sections of the *Acta Sanctorum Bollandiana* (Paris, Palmé, 1863–69).

INDEX